James O. Halliwell

A Viewe of some Part of such publike wants and Disorders as are in the Service of God, etc.

James O. Halliwell

A Viewe of some Part of such publike wants and Disorders as are in the Service of God, etc.

ISBN/EAN: 9783337153861

Printed in Europe, USA, Canada, Australia, Japan

Cover: Foto ©ninafisch / pixelio.de

More available books at **www.hansebooks.com**

A viewe of some part of such publike
wants and disorders as are in the service of God, within her Majesties countrie *of Wales, togither with an humble* PETITION, unto this high Court of Parliament for their speedy redresse.

Anno 1588.

FROM THE ORIGINAL EDITION.

EDITED BY

JAMES O. HALLIWELL, ESQ., F.R.S.

LONDON:
PRINTED BY THOMAS RICHARDS,
37, GREAT QUEEN STREET.
1861.

PREFACE.

The original title-page of the following work runs as follows,—"A viewe of some part of such publike wants and disorders as are in the service of God within her Majesties countrie of Wales, togither with an humble Petition unto this high Court of Parliament for their speedy redresse. Wherein is shewed not only the necessitie of reforming the state of religion among that people, but also the onely way, in regarde of substaunce, to bring that reformation to passe." There is no date, excepting on the half-title to the work itself. The author's preface is addressed " to all those that faythfully love the Lord Jesus, and unfainedly desire the flowrishing estate of Sion." In the course of it, he says,—"It was a common demaund the last Parliament, where the cause of reformation (being then laboured for) was 26 or 28 years agone, and wherfore, after so many years of the Gospell, enjoyed in this land, the motion of altering the outward state of the Church in the offices and officers therof, came it so out of time to be considered off? Least the like objection should be used in the ages to come, behold, the mountayns of Wales do now, in the 31 yeare of the raign of Queen Elizabeth, call heaven and earth to witness that they are weary of their dumb ministers, non-residents, Lord Bishops, &c., and that they desire to be watered by the dewe of Christ's holy Gospell, and to be compassed about with that beautifull wall of his holy government. It were pity indeed but I should intreat the high court of Parliament to heale the disease of my countrie, but so notwithstanding as they would suffer the cause of the griefe and misery thereof still to remaine, the Parliament should be sued unto for helpe against the disease and bane of the country of Wales, but so as they would favor the causes thereof. And what malladie is there, I pray you, in our Church, whereof the dumbe ministers, non-residents, our Lord Bishops, with the rest of that ungodly generation are not the cause. I should spare them who spare not the Church, and in whose eyes the glory of God is not esteemed, and yet the Lord knoweth that I hate them no farther then they are God's enemies. Their favor I desire not as long as they continue to be the adversaries of the Church. If they would yeeld peace unto it, I would be soon brought to lay down my complaints against them. Concerning you, my deare countrimen, whom God, of his infinit goodnes and mercy, hath translated out of the kingdome of darknes unto the blessed possession of the heavenly Jerusalem, I beseech you very earnestly that you would be carefull to walk worthy the Gospel of Christ. Be careful hereof, whether your abode be in England or in Wales, and, at any hand, endevor to live where you may enjoie the meanes of the Word, and be carefull to have the Lord purely worshipped in your families. Particularly, let me here put you in mind, right honourable and worshipfull who of my countreye are in this Parliament, to acquaint this honorable court with the miseries of our country, and to be earnest for a redresse."

It is hardly necessary here to enumerate Penri's other well-known works. The present is selected as the one, perhaps, the most important to those who are interested in the religious history of Wales.

Feb. 1861.

A viewe of some part of such publike
wants and disorders as are in the service of
God, within her Majesties countrie
of Wales, togither with an humble
PETITION, unto this high Court of
Parliament for their speedy redresse.
Anno 1588.

THE æternall God, before whom I nowe stand, and shall stande in that day, eyther to be acquited or condemned; knoweth that the pitifull and miserable estate of my pitifull and miserable countreimen, the inhabitants of Wales; doe inforce me in most dutifull and humble maner, at this time, both to lay open before your eyes, whoe, by the providence of God, are now to be assembled togither in this highe court of parlament: the wantes and deformities of the service of god in wales, my deere and native country, and also to intreat with the like submission, that the same by your wisdomes may be speedely redressed. The Lords holy service amonge that people hath many corruptions and more wants. Their case in regarde therof is very pitifull. Few or none there be who are thorowly touched to have compassion thereof. The means of redresse is in the hands of this assembly, who are met together, to the end that al the subjects of this kingdome, may with fredome and liberty acquaint them with their suits and Petitions, for the promotinge of Gods glory, and the good of their cuntry. And therfore, in that I make known unto this high court, the greefes of my country, and desire the redresse thereof, therin I neither intreat anything which lieth not in your power to grant, nor crave that, wherin the case being neglected by others, I may not lawfully be a suter. The reason that mooveth me thereunto, is the discharge of my duty towards the Lord my God, towards his Church, towardes my native country, and towards you of this honorable assemblie, which coulde not stand with my silence nowe in this suit. Concerning the Lorde, because I am a pore wretched sinner, upon whom he hath shewed great mercies, in pardoning my great offences often committed against his majestie; I have by his grace taken a bonde of my selfe, to seeke the promoting of his honor by al means possible: and in the seeking thereof, to utter the truth as far as my calling wil permit, without respect of person, time, place, estate, or condition of life whatsoever; and so to become an utter enemie unto all these corruptions (by what authoritie or person soever they be maintained) whereby his holy service is hindred. And therfore you of this honorable assembly are not to marvel, that I both seeke the overthrow of these corruptions in Wales, whereof anon I wil speak more at larg, wherby the Lords holy and sacred ministery is shamefully polluted, and his service with the salvation of his people greatly withstood : and also lay uppon you whose authority, good name, credit, estimation, and high place, I ought and by the grace of god wil defend, against al the detractors therof, even with the losse of my life when it shalbe needful; the staine and discredit of denying gods heavenly truth, the passage joyned with the continuance of the lamentable miserie of soules, and the defence of monstrous impietie, even in gods own house, unles you yeeld unto the suit, wherunto at this present you are entreated to be favorable. As for the Church of God into which I have bin begotten thorowe the word preched, by means of my abode in Englande, in these peaceable dayes of her highnes. I have wholly dedicated my selfe to seeke the flowrishing estate thereof by labouring to beautifie the same, both in the plucking up by the rootes, of these filthie Italian weedes, wherwith it is nowe miserably deformed; and planting therein whatsoever might be for the comlines of Gods orchard, in respect of my poore countrey; because it pleased the Lord of life that therin I first sawe the light of the sunne, and have been by my parents there living, brought up in both the universities of this land, to the end if ever the Lord enabled me, I should procure the good of my native countrymen. I have vowed my selfe dutifully to benefite them al the waies I may. And in doing them good, I purpose not to respect mine own quietnes, yea or life, where my death can win them the gospel. And wherein shall stand my deare cuntrimen in any steed, if not by speaking in their behalf then, when their wantes are most pitiful, and they not able, or not willing, to make knowne their miserie? if not in blessing their deaf ears, in removing the stumblinge blocke from before the eies of the blinde? if not in labouringe to bring them to heaven, who of their owne natures should live eternally in a worse place to their woe? Their misery at this day consisting partly, in the great ignorance of God wherein they live, partly in those corruptions and unlawful callings, where by the Church generally within her majesties dominions is pestered; I am nowe with all humilytie to seeke the redresse both of the one and the other at the handes of this honorable assembly. This ignoraunce also, and these corruptions standing as enemies in the way to hinder my bretheren from eternal life, I professe my selfe to seeke their overthrowe and confusion, and by the Lords assistance as longe as I live, never leave either of both, untill the Church of God in Wales be disburdened of suche unnaturall plantes. Concerning you of this honorable assembly, seing I have receaved the former blessings throughe your handes by meanes of the outward peace, whereof hir right excellent majestic hath made the whole land partaker from the Lord, I cannot of conscience; but in most humble submission and reverent manner, put you in minde of the estate wherein you stand before the Lord, unlesse at this your meetinge, there be order taken, for the reforming in Wales of such things as now shalbe made known unto you to be amisse, and you earnestly with all reverence and dutie, entreated to reforme. May it please you therefore to understand, that there is not only such a defect of the service of the everliving God in all the publike meetinges for the most part, of all the inhabitantes of Wales, hir majesties free borne subjects and people: as the most parishes within that cuntry, want the means of salvation, and have wanted the same all this time of her prosperous government: but also that there is such corruptions in that part of Gods service which is established, as the Lords holy and sacred ministerie, with al other ecclesiastical functions, pertayning unto the outward service of God, and the government of his Church, are most intollerablie abused, and prophaned by such as are there tollerated to intermedle with them. And may it please you in like sort, that some order may be taken, whereby the service of God in his pure worship, being as you heare, many waies defective and corrupt among the people, may be without delay restored unto the integritie, which shalbe acceptable in the sight of God, and the meanes of their salvation who professe the same. This most humble and most waightie petition, I am the rather encoraged at this time to prefer, in as much as it doth not only tend to the salvation of many thousandes soules, whom now (alasse) perish in miserable darknes and ignorance, but concerneth the furtherance, which is the point especially to be respected, of the pure and sincere worship of the eternall God. And it is that cause, being my second incouragement, which you of this high court of parliament professe all of you to favour. For who is he that will not professe himself to be the favorer of a suit tending to the honor of God, and the deliverance of men from eternall woe and perdition? And it is that cause, wherein every of you are bound upon your alegeance unto the Lord and her majesty, laying al other maters aside, first and principally to deale; and so to deale as you suffer not your selves, for any worldly respectes, either by the utter rejecting, or by the cold and carelesse intertaining hereof, to betraie God, to betray his truth, to betraie the salvation of men, and to betray the whole kingdome unto the fiery wrath of God's heavie displeasure: Of all which sinnes the Lord himselfe findeth and pronounceth every one of you to be guiltie, that will not labour at this time of your assemblie, for the promoting of the cause nowe in hand. And howesoever in former times, he hath seemed hitherto to wincke at the carelesse respect, which you have had to his true service: yet you are now to understand, that is to be feared, lest shamefull and speedie destruction will betide the whole kingdome, if the suite whereuppon the worshipp of Gods owne

Majestic standeth; be as slenderly entreated of the parliament of England, as alway heretofore it hath bene. And that the petition may appear to be no other, then that, which he by whome alone all kingdoms and common welths are maintained, requireth without contradiction to be graunted, by this honourable assemblie, except his heavie wrath and displeasure, would be procured upon the whole land. And that it may apear to be no other then that, the graunt where of, is the onlie way to save them on whose behalf it is made; no other then that which no state, no kingdom, no councell, prince, potentate, high or lowe can denie, except they would shewe them selves to have no care of religion and pietie: that these thinges I say may appear, we are to consider more at large of the petition, and then whether it be such, as upon the denial thereof, the wrath and anger of God is to be expected, for to fal upon them, who shall denie the same, and the whol land for their sinne. Nowe therefore, if there be nothing else required at your hand, in this whole treatise following, but that which the Lord himselfe from heaven, pronounceth to be so neerly joined with the former points; as upon the refusall of the suite, you shal openly declare, that you are an assembly wherein the Lords cause shal not be hard; an assemblie wherein the felicitie of miserable men shall not be respected; an assembly who wittingly and willingly call for the judgments of God upon the whole kingdome; an assembly wherein trueth, **religion**, and pietie can beare no swaye: then I hope that none will be found in this honorable court, to be such an enemie unto the honor of God, the felicitie of men, and the quiet state of this common wealth: none so prophane, wicked, and irreligious, as even to thinke that the consultation of this matter may be differred. But if on the other side, the suite be founde to be of no such importance, as before is expressed, or if I be found to write any thing impertinent unto the former points, or not to have behaved my selfe so dutifull in my stile and manner of writing towards this honorable court, as it became the basest vassel under heaven, having a calling to deale in the like cause, to carie himself towardes the princes of his people, then let not my life be precious in your sight. Here therefore, with all humility and reverence, before the eternall God, his elect Angels and Church, her right excellent, our dread soveraigne, Queene Elizabeth; I call everye one of you to recorde, that upon the perill of my life, I will shewe, that you cannot but give care unto the suite, which is now preferred unto you, though by my base and sinnefull hands, except you will neglect the honor of God, set light by the salvation of his people, endanger the state of her Majesty (whom the Lord long preserve unto his glorie) with the whole kingdome, and proclaime unto the world, that all religion and truth is perished from amonge you. My manner of dealing herein, as it shalbe by the grace of God in all dutie and submission; as writing unto those, whose authoritie and places, I am not without great reverence to consider, so shal it be plaine and free without minishing or clipping any part of the trueth (for the feare or favor of any creature) which it concerneth you to heare; wherein I will utter nothing but that, which by the assistance of God, I will scale with my blood, if I shall be driven thereunto. The reason mooving me to so free and plaine a kind of writing, as neither I dealing in the same cause, nor yet any els before me have used, is not (the Lord is my witnes) because I would hereby, arrogate unto my selfe, the prayse of a bolde rebuker of states, and great personages; but it is first, because I deale in that matter, upon the goodnes whereof, I may presume to speak the whole truth of God, especially writing unto an assembly professing true religion. Secondly, because the suite is put up unto them, who although they professe to seeke the honor of God: yet have heretofore altogether undutifully refused to give the hearing unto any motion tending unto the reformation of the religion, which they pretend to favor and professe. Some of them thinking the cause at all not worthie to be delt in. Others, not altogether disliking the suite, judged notwithstanding the time wherein it was to be handled, not to be as yet come. Because they saw that the base and supplicatorie maner whereby it desired the hearing, made al other causes comming with authority from men, to be preferred before it. The most who in deede sincerely favoreth the cause, have thought it to be a gainles matter to deale at all therein. For as much as it is the generall voyce of all men, that reformation cannot be taken in hand, without the high and heavie displeasure of her Majestie, who (to speake as I am perswaded) being borne in hand, by the ungodly perswasions of some godlesse and irreligious men of the Ecclesiastical state, that the Church within her Majesties dominions, cannot be at a better stay then it is; hath not without great reason, bene hitherto the hardliar induced to have the cause of religion againe dealt in, which she is perswaded altogether to be in a tollerable sort, according to the will of her God. Being also undutifully borne in hand that the endevour of reforming religion is nothing else, but a new fangled and seditious attempt, proceeding from the factious and discontented braines of those, who are slandered to desire thereby nothing els, but the alteration of the present state, dangerous to her royal crowne and person, and ruinous unto the whole kingdome. In respect whereof, the cause offering it selfe againe to be considered of this high court; it became the same to come, with a majesticall and terrifying countenance; that if it pleased the Lorde, it might this way for feare compell them dutifully to stoupe unto it, whose favor and good liking in a peaceable manner, hitherto it coulde by no means procure. And it became it so to offer it selfe, as withall it might appeare, that the enterprise of reforming religion, is not a matter tendinge to the disturbinge of the commonwealth, and the disliking of her Majestie. Except men would slanderously surmise the estate of this kingdome, to be so out of square, as Gods trueth cannot have passage therein, without the imminent ruine of al, and slanderously report her Majesties will and affection, to be then intollerably crossed, when the will of her God, is sought to be established: which assertions, shalbe manifested to be grievous, and undutifull slaunders against hir Majestic and the state; by the opening of such thinges as being amisse within Wales, the Lorde requireth to be reformed, at the handes of her Majestie and this Parliament.

The wants therefore, and corruptions of the service of God in Wales, joyned with the misery of that people are; first, in that the most congregations within that countrie, have all this time of the Gospell preached in Englande, had no other service of God, for the working of fayth and repentance sounding in them, but such, as whereby the people partaking the same, cannot possibly be saved ordinarily. Mistake me not. For I doe not saye, that eyther that service, which all this time of her Majesties goverment they have had, and now have, is idolatrous, or that by the publike authoritie of her Majestie and the Parliament, they have bin publikely enjoyned, to professe any other religion, then that only true religion, in the profession whereof alone, ordinary salvation is to be had. But I affirme that God is not otherwise served in the most assemblies there, then that way, whereby the food of eternall life shall never be ordinarily convayed to the people. This I affirme, and this I will stand unto, because for the space nowe of 30 yeares complete, they have every where, for the most part, wanted the preaching of the word, without which, as it is plainely set downe in manye places of the word,* and I have elswhere largely prooved unto her Majestie and this high court, ordinarily, no fleshe can be saved. Now, my Lords, and you the rest of this Parliament, consider I pray you, what care hath bin had of the soules of men under her Majesties governement, and how in the dayes of reckoning and account these things wil be answered. Consider how lamentable a case it is, that in the flowrishingest government for outward peace, that is again under the cope of heaven; where publike idolatrie hath bene banished, not one family or one tribe; but a whole nation should perishe for want of knowledge. And see whether I have not sufficient cause to deale with you on the behalfe of my countrie. My crie, my crie is not the crie of (Deut.

* Jam. 1. 12; 1 Pet. 1. 21; Job 33. 23; 1 Cor. 1. 21; Rom. 10. 14; Ephes. 1. 13; and 2. 17; Acts 20. 32; Pro. 8. 34, 35; Isay. 53. 12.

11. 8) giltlesse and innocent blood, which were verye woefull, but of lost and damned soules, which is most lamentable: and give you eare unto it, my LL. least the blood of soules bee laide to your charge, and required at your hands. For it is not the indispensible dutie of the Parliament to give eare unto this crie? Howe then I praye you, will it be answered before the judge of all the worlde in the day of judgement, if you be carelesse of a dutie so necessarily required at your handes: when our Saviour Christ affirmed it (Luk. 9. 22) to be nothing availeable unto men, to winne the whole worlde, if they lose their owne soules. Did he thereby, thinke you, not only enforce that they are in a miserable taking, who in respect of the knowledge of their salvation, know not the right hand from the left: but also forcible in feare, that governours unto whome of trust he hath committed inferiours, discharge not their duties in his sight, unlesse they have great care of the salvation of their people? Questionlesse he doth. Let them therefore be afraide of æternall shame and confusion, who blushe not to be busie in the consultation of everye trifling matter, and would be accounted great state men for tything Minte and Cummin, whereas in the meane time, they are not ashamed, no not to withstande the consultation, purposing to bring that to passe, which the wisdome of God himselfe Jesus Christ, hath pronounced to be worthy the whole world, even

the saving health of men. Wel the day will come, how soone he alone knoweth, in whose handes are the keyes of all knowledge; wherein it shall appeare by wofull experience, and that too late, what an heavie reckoning will bee made with such Parliament men. And take you heed that are of this assembly, now at the length after so many warnings, lest you be found in their number, who make light account of the cause of the Gospell offered unto them, and who thinke the matter of mens salvation, to be nothing else but a conceit, wherewith the immaginations of melanchollicke heads are usually troubled. The cause one day shalbe found worth the consideration, howsoever men now thinke that they may without dammage securely contemne the same. And I woulde humbly intreate this high courte more seriously to consider thereof. The suite is, that Gods honour may be truely yeelded unto him by the subjectes of this kingdome, and that their soules may be saved in the daye of Jesus Christ; such a suit as a greater cannot be consulted of amongst the sonnes of men. And will not the wisest and greatest assembly in the land, take order that this may be harkened unto? Wil they not consult of a waye how men may come unto the means whereby they may be saved; to what end else, my Lordes, should you be assembled together, if this cause be not handled in your meetings? A Parliament gathered together in England, in the dayes of the Gospell under Queene Elizabeth, and the cause of Gods honor, and the felicitie of the subjectes never thought upon, never accounted worthy the consultation. Such a state and such a government may flowrish and continue in peace for a time: but undoubtedly the destruction therof is decreed with the Lord, the execution of which decree, shal not be overlong deferred, without speedie repentance. Can there be a meeting of all states in the lande to consult in Parliament, what may be most behoffull for the promoting of Gods glorye, and the good of the commonwelth, and yet no care had, how the æternal miserie of a whole nation, even almost the fourth part of the kingdome may be prevented? What is this else but to dally with Gods honour, and to delude his people of their salvation? When especially after so many Parliaments, in a kingdome freely professing the Gospell for the space of 30. yeares, in the fourth part of the kingdome, there shalbe founde such grosse ignorance, as no region under heaven, coulde at anye time yeelde the like president, so long after the bannishing of idolatrie. I doe not solace my self in considering the miserie of my native cuntrimen, neither do I thinke thereof at all, unlesse it be to bewaile their estate, and to consider how it may be redressed. This I may say of them without offence, that they never as yet for the most part, enjoyed the preaching of the Gospell, since they wer professed idolators under poperie. Now what felicitie concerning spirituall things, a profession without the Gospell preached can have, the same they may enjoye I denie not. But what will be the end of such a profession? verely even this. After a few dayes miserably spent in this life such professors shalbe sure (for any thing that is otherwise revealed) to live in hell for evermore. Will it then profit them at all, to have lived in a kingdome professing true religion, though they have gayned the whol world therein, seeing they are sure to lose their owne soules: because in this life they have wanted the preaching of the Gospell. And if this that I have set downe be not sufficient to expresse their miserie, and to moove you to consider of them, I know not what may be accounted miserable, or what may procure compassion. Or if this will not moove you to graunt them the preaching of the Gospell, then shal you leave unto posterities, but a small testimonie of your religious hearts, and love to the Lords sanctuarie. Is there not an heaven my Lordes, after this life for men to goe unto? Is it possible that they shall ordinarily go thither, who never enjoyed the preaching of the Gospell? Or can our people in Wales looke for extraordinarie salvation? And will not you see that they be no longer destitute of this meanes, whereby they may walk in the statutes of life and not die? Is this peticion that God may be truly honored, and the soules of men saved, hurtful to the state, dangerous to her Majesties crowne and dignitie, and contrary unto hir affection? cannot this state stand if God should be truly honored, and that people trained in the waies of godlines? Cannot her Majesties crowne and dignitie stand, if these thinges be enacted in Parliament? And must shee needs be undutifully gainsaid, when the honor of her God, and the blessednesse of her people are pleaded for? Whosoever have, do, or will slaunder their soveraigne, and the whole state, in this vile and undutifull sort, it is pitie they were not severely punished. Againe, my LL., is that a religious assembly? Is that an assemblie wherein trueth, pietie, the honor of God, and the æternall happinesse of men shal beare any sway, where this petition can not be granted? Which desireth nothing els, but that whiche may be enacted without the great hurt of any, and which ought to be graunted, whatsoever in the judgment of fleshly wise men might seeme to ensue thereof. They will never therefore in the sight of God and his Churche, escape the ignominie and staine of irreligious and profane men, whose eyes will not be mooved with compassion at the estate of our people, and defects of Gods service among them. Nowe if I be thought to have reported any untrueth, concerning their estate, let me be brought face to face, for the triall hereof, with those unto whom the care (I should say the spoile) of the Church there is committed, and being convinced to have uttered any untrueth, let me have no favour, but dye the death, before you of this honourable assemblye, and my blood be upon my owne heade, for impeaching the credite of the rulers of my people and their governement, undutifully by publike writing, whose estimation I know it to be unlawfull for me, even in thought once to violate.

I doe here therefore before your Hh. offer to proove more at large, that the most congregations in Wales, want the very especiall outwarde markes of a Church, and so the meanes of salvation by the worde preached, and the comfort of fayth, by the right administration of the Sacraments. I also offer to proove, that your Hh. without your speedie repentaunce, shalbe reckoned with, because that in this point, you have plowed but iniquitie, and sowed wickednes, and so as Job sayth, you shall reape the same (Job 4. 8). Beleeve them not, who tell you that all is well within Wales, and that they are a sort of clamorous and undiscreet men, who affirme the contrary. Beleve them not, who tell you that it belongeth not unto your duties to be carefull of the estate of the Church, and that the Lorde requireth no more at your hands, but the mayntenance of outwarde peace. As though men committed to your governement, were but droves of bruite beastes, onely to be foddered, and kept from external invasions and inroods. Give eare rather unto the words of the Prophet (Je. 17. 13. 14.) who with a loude voyce crieth unto you; Why will you die, you, your families and people, by the sword, by the famine, and by the pestilence. And why will you be damned (I may alude without injurie unto the word) as the Lord hath spoken against all those governours, that wil not see their people provided* for, of the meanes of salvation. Therefore heare not the words of the prophets, who tell you, that you shall neyther see sword nor famine, though you be still as careles of your people, as hitherto you have bene. Looke the punishments both of flattering prophetes, and of those that are deceived by their flatterie. Jerem. 14. 15. Heare them not I say, but obeye the Lord in the execution of that dutie which he exacteth at your hands, by calling your people to the knowledge of his sonne, that you may live. For why should this lande be made desolate, for this your carelesnes? Jerem. 27. 17. They prophesie vanitie and lies unto you, which saye peace, peace, while you dispise the Lorde, and walke in this secure course, or else Jeremiah is deceived. If they be prophets, and if the word of the Lord be in their mouths, let them intreat her Majestie, and you of this parliament, that the misery of helples Wales, may at this time of your meeting be considered off, and redressed.

Thus I have set downe some part of the wants in the service of God in Wales, and some part of that

---

* Ezra 7. 17, 23; Psa. 2. 10; and 101; 2 Chron. 29. 10; and 30. 9; and 34; 27. ex. 20. 10; Gen. 18. 19; 2 Chr. 15. 12; 13. and 17. 7.

miserie, wherein my countrie is bewrapped; and which you are bound unto the Lord (but by me most humbly entreated) to redresse. And this is the cause wherein if you deale not, you betray the honor of God, betraye his trueth, betraye the religion which you professe, and betraye her Majestie, and the whole kingdome, unto the revenging hand of God. For without controversie, the continuance of our ignorance, and the defectes of Gods service, will one day, and that shortly, I feare me, bring the Lord in fearefull and consuming judgements to take punishment of you, your wives, children, families and the whol land: because in your states and consultation, his honor, and the blood of mens souls were not regarded. But this is neyther all the miserie of the inhabitants of Wales, neyther is this all that the Lorde requireth to be amended by this Parliament, under paine of his heavie wrath.

In the seconde place then we are to consider, the corruptions tollerated by the positive lawes of this land, and countenanced by the authority of this high court of Parliament, in the service of God within Wales. Whereby no small dishonor redoundeth unto the Majestie of God, and wherein no small part of the spirituall miserie of that people doth consist. For the removing of which corruptions, it behoveth the Parliament, with speede to be very carefull, even before such time as the Lord calleth the land to an account, for the wicked constitutions therein maintayned. Here therefore I affirme, unlesse without delay you labour to cleanse the Churche under your governement in Wales, of all L.Bb. dumbe ministers, nonresidents, archdeacons, commissaries, and all other romish officers and offices, there tollerated, and so tollerated, as by the consent and authoritie of the Parliament they are mainteyned; that you are both in this life and the life to come, likely to be subjecte unto the intollerable masse of Gods wrath, the execution whereof is not unlikely to fall upon you and your houses, unlesse you prevent the fiercenes of the Lordes indignation.

If Moses by a positive law, should have allowed the offring of strange fire by Nadab and Abihu, tollerated the ministery of blemished and deformed Levites (Lev. 20. 18-23); enacted that one, not being of the line of Aaron, might presse before the Altar, (Num. 16. 10; 18. 7) to offer the bread of his God: if David had made it lawfull for Uzzah, to lay his hand upon the Arke; if Josiah or any other the godly rulers had, either given leave to the cursed shepheardes in their dayes, to place others in their stead, to take the oversight of the Sanctuary? (Ezek. 44. 9.) Or permitted a consecrated priest to be a civill governour; briefely had established any thing in the Churche goverment prescribed by Moses, contrary to the commandement, had they not bene in danger of the Lords wrath? They had without controversie.

And shall you of the high court of Parliament be dispenced with, being guilty (except you labor to remove the dumbe ministery, nonresidence, with the usurped and Antichristian seats of L. Bb. &c.) of tollerating and establishing greater sinnes among your people in Wales, in steed of the government prescribed by Jesus Christ? assure your selves no. I do therefore in this point also, for the discharge of my dutie and conscience towardes the Lord, his Church, my countrie, and the whol estate of this kingdom, taking my life in my hand testifying unto you, before the Majestie of God, and before his church, that our dumbe ministers, that the callings of our L. Bb. archdea. commiss. with al other remnants of the sacriledge brought into the Churche by that Romishe strumpet, and now remaining in Wales, are intollerable before the Lorde, and that it is not likely that ever you tollerating these thinges any longer, shall escape Gods fierie wrath. The trueth hereof I do briefly make knowne by the reasons following, and offer to proove them more at large, even upon the peril of my life, against our 4. L. Bb. all their chaplains, retainers, favorers and welwillers; whether in eyther of the two universities of this lande, or in any place els whatsoever. These things I offer to proove against M. D. Bridges, who lately in a large volume, hath undertaken their defence. In which booke of his, he hath offered her Majestie and the Parliament most undutifull injurie, by going about for the maintenance of his owne belly, and the belies of the rest of his coat, to allienat the hears of the loyallest subjects in the lande, from their most carefull prince and governours. As though her Majestie and this honourable court, ment to turne the edge of the sword against them, who indeed deserve not to be threatned with the scabbord. Into which booke he hath crammed as plaine poperie for the defence of our Bb. as ever Harding, Saunders, Turrian, Bellarmine, or any other the firebrands and ensigne bearers of Romish treason against her Majesties crowne, have brought for the Popes supremacie.* And for as much as he in that booke, hath both undertaken the defence of those corruptions, for the tollerating wherof the anger of God hangeth over the whole land; and also shewed himselfe to be Ammonitish Tobiah, against the buylding of Jerusalem in Wales, by defending the very breaches and ruins of the Babylonish overthrow, which by the just judgements of God under poperie we sustained, to be the perfectest building that Sion can be brought unto; and so by this slander withstandeth the salvation (which I doubt not) her Majestie and the parliament wishe unto my country. I have so framed the reasons following, as they overthrow the very foundation and whole frame of that wicked book and of al

* Compare pag. 448 of D. Bridges his booke with Bellarmine. cap. 10. li. 5. cont 3. and you shall finde the one to have writen the verie same thing for the Arch. that the other hath for the pope.

others, written for the defence of our established Church government.

Now that our dumbe ministers, nonresidents, L. bishops, archdea. &c. are nothing els but an encrease of sinnefull men, (Num. 22. 14) risen up in steed of their fathers the idolatrous Monkes and Fryars, stil to augment the fierce wrath of God against this land and our governors: and that this booke of D. Bridges, and whatsoever els hath bin written for their defence, are nothing els, but edicts, trayterous against God, and slanderous to your sacred government, to defend the sale and exchange of Church goods, and the very destruction of souls: to speak al in a word, that both these corruptions and their defences, are condemned by the Lords own revealed wil, as things directly against the same, and the lawes of her Majestie, expressed in his written word; and therefore not to be tollerated by your authoritie, unlesse you thinke that you may tollerate sinne by your lawes; nor yet once to be spoken for or countenaunced, unlesse you would plead for Baal, I proove by these reasons. (Judg. 6. 31.)

That forme of Church governement whiche maketh our Saviour Christ inferior unto Moses, is an impious, ungodly, and unlawfull goverment flat contrarye to the worde, (Heb. 3. 6; Nom. 12. 7) and therefore in no case to be tollerated by any lawes or authoritie, and the booke or bookes defending the same, are ungodly and impious bookes. But our Churche government in Wales, by L. bishops, archd. dumb ministers, and other ecclesiastical officers (as for nouresidents, let this one reason for all serve against them; they as much as in them lieth, bereave the people over whome they thrust themselves, of the onely ordinarie meaus of salvation, which is the word preached) is such goverment, as maketh the Lord of life, Jesus Christ, inferiour to Moses, and this booke of D. Bridges, with all other bookes of the like arguments doe the same. Therfore this government is a government, not to be tollerated by law in any state, unlesse men woulde feele Gods heavie judgementes for the same, and therefore also it is a government most pernicious and dangerous, even in pollicie unto the civil government where it is established, and this booke or books defending the same, are ungodly, wicked and pernicious bookes, trayterous against the Majestie of Jesus Christe; crying for unsufferable vengeance upon such as tolerate them.

The proposition is not to be doubted off. For is that Church government or bookes to be tollerated, which make Christ Jesus, the sonne of the æternall God, yea God himselfe, inferiour unto Moses? The assumption is thus prooved. That governement, and that booke or bookes, whiche holdeth Jesus Christ God and man, to have prescribed no externall forme of the government of his Churche; but such, as at the pleasure of the magistrate, when time and place requireth,

E

may be altered without sinne ; preferreth Moses before Jesus Christe. This is manifest out of the expresse wordes of the text Heb. 3. 2. 6. Because the Lord Jesus, being the sonne, is in that place compared with Moses a faithfull servant in deed, and preferred before Moses, in regard of the external government, which Moses had so faythfully prescribed under the law, as it was not to be chaunged at the pleasure of any magistrate, untill the Messiah should cause the oblations to cease. (Dan. 9. 27.) For what king was there ever in Judah, who without the breach of Gods law, could alter the external regiment of the Jewish Church in the Levitical priesthood and officers? (1 Chron. 23. 24.) David, I grant, ordained some things not mentioned in the bookes of Moses, but that whiche he did, proceeded from the spirit of God, and he had the worde for his warrant. The same is to be saide of whatsoever was done by any other of the godly kings in Judah.

Nowe that the former comparison, Heb. 3. 2. 6. betweene the sonne and the servant, Christe and Moses, is concerning the externall regiment of the church, and not the spiritual government of the inner man (as D. Bridges affirmeth pag. 51. line 30.) it is plaine. Because Moses had nothing to do with the governing of the inner man ; and therefore it were no prerogative for the Lorde to be preferred in faithfulnes before Moses, in that dispensation wherein Moses never dealt. Hence then I assume, that our forme of Church government in Wales, and this wicked booke, holdeth Jesus Christ to have ordained such an externall forme of government in his Churche, at his departure from earth to heaven, as at the pleasure of the magistrate, might be altered without the breach of Gods institution: which thing D. Bridges affirmeth pag. 55. And all our prelates grant that this high court of parliament may lawfully alter the forme of Church governement now established. Therefore this government, and this booke, preferreth Moses before Jesus Christ. And I cannot see how far this differeth from blasphemie. Now if Christ should be saide to ordaine no externall regiment at all, then Moses was far before him, and the thirst of superioritie in our prelates, and their accomplisses, is turned into extreame drunkennes of impietie by this assertion.

I beseech the Lord in mercy to open your eies that are of this assemblie, that you may see how he and his people have been dealt with by retaining such laws in force, as justle and overthrow the roial prerogative of his sonn. And the Lord make you to see whether those men, that defend the interest of the sonn of God in this point against the tiranicall usurpation of Bb. and have brought for his title unanswerable evidence, out of the sacred records of Gods owne writings, offending eyther in matter or circumstance in no one thing, but that they have not dealt more earnestlie with your Hh. and more roundly with the adversaries in the right of their master; have deserved to be imprisoned, thruste out of their livinges, reviled, and railed upon by ungodly and wicked prelats unto the state, as seditious and discontented men with the civil government, dangerous subjectes and enimies unto her Majesties crown. And surely the cause being made knowne unto you, as nowe it is, how soever the Lord may beare with your oversight heretofore, in the ignoraunce of the waight thereof: yet if you doe not, nowe abrogate such a church government, well may you hope for the favour and intertainement of Moses, that is the curse of the lawe: but the favoure and loving countenance of Jesus Christ, I doe not see how you shal ever enjoy. To prosecute this point a little farther. In most humble manner, I would know of you that are of this high court, whether of these 2 pointes following you would be said to maintain, by the continuance of the aforesaid callings, and corruptions within Wales? For of either of the 2 you must needes be guiltie. First doe you thinke you may presume to defend by your authoritie and lawes, such offices and officers in the ecclesiastical state, whereby the churche is to be governed; that is, such a Church government, as in your consciences you cannot but acknowledg to be unlawful before the Lord, and hurtful unto his Church? Secondly, doe you thinke that any Church government can be lawfull before your God, and profitable unto his church, which the Lord Jesus Christ himself hath not prescribed in his word? The which point whosoever goeth about to defend, he, as before you have hard, maketh Jesus Christ, who as he is the onely head of his churche, so he hath the alone jurisdiction to ordaine the goverment thereof, not to have in the goverment of his owne house as great a prerogative as Moses had. I earnestlie intreat you then, that as you would not be accounted, ether to defend and countenance those things which in your owne consciences are sinful, or to account such a Church government to be lawful, as cannot stand with the roiall soverainty, that Jesus Christ hath in his church: so to see the spedy abolishing of al dumbe ministers, Lorde Bishops, Archdeacons, commissaries, chauncellors, &c. out of the church, under your government in Wales. You are now intreated to abrogate no other Church goverment then that, which either in your own consciences you must acknowledg to be unlawful and odious in the sight of God, and therefore without delay to be removed, or such a regiment the unlawefulnes whereof, if with our Bishops you should go about to maintaine, then should you rob Jesus Christ of the prerogative and priveledge wherewith the spirit of God hath adorned him. Heb. 3. 6. Because it hath been shewed, that it was not lawful for any state or power to ordaine any other forme of government in the church under the lawe, then that prescribed by Moses. If then you think our church government by

Lord Bb. Archdeacons, dumb ministers, &c.: in your consciences to be unlawful, that is; if you think it unlawful for a minister to joine the office of a civil Magistrate with his ministerie, and to beare rule and dominion over his bretheren, either as a spiritual or temporal Lord; if you think it unlawfull for a Lord Bishop to beare soveraigne authoritie of al the ministers within his diocesse; and if you think it un-unlaweful that their ministerie with the execution thereof, should depend upon his plesure, or disliking; if also in your conscience you think it unlawful for him to take the charge of al the soules within 4. or 5. shires, and to take the charge of those mens soules, whose faces for the most part, he wel knoweth he shal never behold; if in like manner you think it unlawfull for an Archdeacon, whose name and office was never read of in the word, and in his best institution is but to atend upon the ministers and looke unto the poore (to have a great number of ministers at his becke and controlment) or if you think it unlawful in your soules and consciences, for our dumb ministers, the patrons of al ignorance and blindenes, to take upon them the office of the imbassadors of Jesus Christ, to declare his will unto the people, the best part whereof, they themselves never know: then there is no question to be made, but that either you wil utterly raze the memorie of this wicked and ungodly generation out of the Churche of Wales, or openly manifest, unto men and angels, that you will to the contumelious dishonor of your God, and the undoing of his church, countenance and maintaine L. Bishops, Archdeacons, dumbe ministers, with the rest of that ungodly race, whose corruptions in youre owne consciences you cannot but detest. On the other side, if you think it lawful for you, to ordain, what forme of church government you like best of: and so holde it lawful for to maintaine this established among us; then see what wil follow the diminishinge of the prerogative that Jesus Christ hath in the government of his church. And that I feare me wil be this. The Lord will enter into judgement with you of this parliament, for al the soules that hereafter shal be damned in Wales. Because you make it lawfull by your authority, for such guides to be over your people, as cannot possiblie lead, and direct them in the waies of godlines and salvation. He wil enter into judgment with you for al the sinnes that shalbe commited, for want of goverment, which his son Christ hath ordained as a meanes to keepe men from transgressing against their God. He will enter into judgment with you for the monstrous profanation, whereby those proude, popelike, and blinde guides, have polluted his house in the dayes of your government, which you shoulde have withstood. He wil enter in to judgment with you for the punishments that are likely to fall upon them, because you have countenanced, and freely priveleadged them by lawe, to provoke his wrath in that grevous sort against their own souls. He wil alsoe (it is to be feared) enter into judgement with the whol land, for this your sinne, and make his sword drunk with the bloud of our slain men, yea he wil give the whole kingdom, high and lowe, into the handes of the enemie, that is cruel and skilful to destroy, that all the nations under heaven professing religion, may feare and take heed, howe they doe not only denye to be governed by the lawes of his sonne Jesus Christ, but which is more grievous in stead thereof, establishe such institutions as are directly against his majesties revealed will. If those thinges be not likely to fall uppon us, except the above mencioned unlawfull callings of Lord Bb. dumbe ministers, &c. be now at once even in this Parliament rooted out of the churche in Wales, let not my head go to the grave in peace. Where are they now, who usually affirm the intent or motion of removing L.Bb. dum ministers, ye the whol church goverment established in Wales, to be a matter odious in the sight of her Majestie, and dangerous to the state? Cannot hir Majesty abide to heare, that Christ Jesus should be more faythful in his owne house, then Moses was? Is it an odious hearing unto her Majestie, that the churche in her kingdome should be cleansed of al unlawful callings and corruptions, and beutified, with the holy ordinances of her saviour Jesus Christ, even in her daies; that the same praise might be trulie ascribed unto hir, in the adges to come, which the spirite of God hath yeeled unto King Josiah. (2. Kin. 23. 25.) Like unto Queene Elizabeth was there no Queene before hir, that turned unto the Lord with all hir hart, with all her soule, and with al hir might, according to all the lawe of Moses, neither after hir arose ther any like unto hir. Cannot hir Majestie, I say, abide these things? Far be it that any should perswade them selves she cannot. Then are they undutiful slaunderers of hir highnes, who to terrifie the Parliament from dealing, concerninge the redresse of the church, usually avouch such purposes, to be altogether vaine, because hir Majestie will never be induced to yeeld hir consent unto the removing of the established governement of the Church; neither is the slaunder any whit lesse undutifull against the state, when the kingdome is said to be indangered, except Jesus Christ, should make it lawfull for the Parliament to tollerate what Church government the civill state can best away with. And it is a point wherin you of this Parliament may shew what harts you beare unto the sinceritie of religion. My 2 reason followeth.

That forme of Church government, and that booke or bookes, which make the established regiment to be an humaine constitution, that is inclusively according to the worde (but no otherwise according to the worde then the civill governement is, whiche also must bee

F

inclusively according to the same,) (1. Pet. 2. 13; 2. Pet. 2. 10.) and so may at the pleasure of man bee altered, as the civill governement may: that government and that booke or bookes, (besides that they prefer Moses before Jesus Christ) is a wicked and pernicious government, and they ungodly and pestelent bookes. (Pag. 55.)

But our Church government in Church causes, and this booke of D. Bridges with al other books of this grieste, make the ecclesiasticall government to be nothing else, but an humane constitution, which may be lawfully altered, and abolished at the magistrates pleasure. Therefore our Church government in Wales, and this booke or bookes, are ungodly and wicked.

The proposition is proved by these resons. First they are wicked and intollerable, because they make no difference between that which belongeth to the true worship of God, as ecclesiasticall government doth, and that which apertaineth unto civil pollicie. Contrarie to the apostle Peter, who affirmeth in expresse wordes, that wee have reaceaved by the knowledge of God, whatsoever belongeth unto true religion, in such sort as it is unlawful for man to add any thing of his owne invention thereunto. For soe the worde *Eusebeia* translated, godlines, signifieth in that place. Whereas the worde hath not so furnished us, with whatsoever belongeth to the civil magistracie, called mans ordinaunce by the same apostle (Pet. 3. 13.), but that

High Court of Parliament. 35

therein those thinges, that have been and are invented by them that never knew God, are warrantable, and may be inclusively according to the word. Secondly ecclesiasticall government being granted to be an human constitution, maketh the Pope to have sufficient warrant out of the word, not of his Idolatrous and false religion, but of his superioritie, over all civil Majestrates and pastors within the ecclesiastical bodie of the church.* For whic should not the pope, the civill Majestrate, granting him this superioritie, (as all they under his jurisdiction doe) be alowed by the word, to be above the emperor, and all other Magistrates and ministers whatsoever, if the ecclesiasticall government be an human ordinance? For I am assured that the emperor, with al other princes in Europe, may lawfully chuse a Magistrate superior unto them all, if they wil. And why may not this magistrate whom they may lawfully chuse (and he lawfully yeelde unto their choyse) to be the highest and superiour governor in christendome, to be a bishop, or an archb. if the Church governement be an humane ordinaunce, or if it be lawfull for either of them to be Lordes, and to beare a civill office? Before I goe farther, I am particularly in this poynt, to deale with such in this parliament, as are our L.Bb. in Wales. Here therefore in the audience of her R. excellent

---

* If you read D. Bridges, pag. 448, line 3, you shall finde him not far from avouching this point.

Majestie, and this honorable councel, I proove before you the B. of Landaff, Davids, Asaph and Bangor, that the Pope of Rome, whose superioritie all sounde hearted christians doe acknowledge to be intollerable and accursed, hath altogether as good warraunt from the worde for his ecclesiasticall hierarchie, as you, unto whom I now speake, to be L.bishops in Wales. My reason I conclude after this manner; and if you can infringe anye part thereof, I will not refuse anye death, or other punishment, that shalbe laide upon me. What Bb. soever they be, that have no other warrant of their lordly jurisdiction, whereby they exercise temporal government, as civil magistrates, having still their ministery upon them, and claime unto themselves superiority over their felow brethren, as ministers, then the ordinance, good will and pleasure of man, that is, of the state wherein they live; they have no better warrant from the word of god, for this their lordly superiority, then the Pope of Rome hath for his, who claymeth no other jurisdiction and superioritie unto himselfe, over magistrats and ministers, then that which he hath, by the free consent, good liking, and authoritye of those states, who voluntarilye submit themselves unto his idolatrous religion. But you the Bb. of Landaff, Davids, Bangor, and Assaph in Wales, have no other warrant to be L.bishops, that is, to joyne both magistracie and ministerie together, and claime unto your selves authority spirituall (in deed according to the spirite that ruleth in the ayre, as the Apostle sayth) over your fellowe ministers, then the constitutions of man, to witt; the will and pleasure of her Majesty and this high court of parliament. Therfore you the said L.bishops, have no other warrant for your Lordships and superioritie over other ministers, then the pope hath for his supream authoritie, and universall prerogative. As for his crueltie, pride, and idolatrous profession; far be it, but I should make difference betweene you and him. Although every part of this reason be already prooved; yet I demand of you, by what authoritie you are so far, in respect of temporal things, and the abuse of ecclesiasticall jurisdiction, preferred before many godly and learned ministers in this land; as you by vertue of your places, are Barons of the parliament house, enjoye great revenews, and are Lordes over your brethren and fellow ministers? Your answere will be, I knowe, that you hold this by sole authoritie of man, and no otherwise. This must needs be your aunswere. For if you woulde claime your jurisdiction by any other title, your bishoppricks would soone be forfeited. Now I pray you tell me, hath not the pope as good warraunt for his hierarchie as this is? For hath not the Emperor, the king of Spain, the Frenche king, with other states, now professing poperie, as good allowance from the worde, in regard of the office (as for the abuse in the person or religion, that is not the question) to make whom they will the superior B. within their owne dominions, as her Majestie and the parliament hath to make one of you to be above al the ministers in your dioces, or as good warraunt as they might have to make eyther of you to be Primate and Metropolitane over the rest; which authoritie you will not denie unto them as unlawfull, I am sure. Eyther, therefore, the superiour power of the pope in his universall bishoppricke, is a lawfull superioritie, or els your lordships having no better warrant from the word, then the popedom hath, are unlawfull, and intollerable. And it being unlawfull for the parliament to tollerate, and countenance (I doe not say the popishe religion) but his superiority over the ministers within this land; it is also as unlawful for them to tollerat your spirituall jurisdiction over your fellow brethren. Here then I appeale unto your consciences, whether you doe not see that the pope hath altogether, as good allowaunce from the worde, of his Antichristian jurisdiction, as you have of your lordly callings. And againe I appeale unto you, whether you, who dare not, but holde the popedome of the B. of Rome to be an unlawfull jurisdiction; do not you thinke, that the pope (though hee professed the trueth of religion, as you doe, which in the dayes of the first bishopps of Rome they also did) were not bounde in conscience, to give over this universall soveraigntie? Or if he coulde not abide to heare, that his place and office, whiche by the positive law, and the good lyking of the present governement, were authorized, shoulde nowe be accounted unlawfull in the sight of God; do you not thinke that hir Majesty, and this high court of parliament, notwithstanding the lawes established, and the favour they beare unto his jurisdiction, were bounde before the Lorde, to abrogate his superioritie, as unlawfull and intollerable in Gods Church. If you thus judge of the pope, as I hope you do! Oh then, why wil not you execute this sentence against your selves, whiche you have pronounced against him? you beeing no lesse guiltie of tyrannizing over your brethren, by vertue of your unlawful calling. The jurisdiction of the pope is unlawful (say you) notwithstanding all the states in Europe alow him to be universall bishop, and it is unlawful notwithstanding poperie were true religion, and hee a most holy man who sate in the Romishe chaire. And you holde it also unlawfull for the parliament, notwithstanding al the former exceptions, to tollerate the popish supremacie, even over the ministers in this land. Why the worde of God by the same reason, pronounceth your callings to be unlawful, and denieth it to be possible for them to be lawfull and tollerable, no though her Majestie and al the states and parliaments in the world ratified them to be lawful.

To returne againe unto the whole bodie of this honourable assemblye. I intreate you in the name of

God to consider, how prejudiciall it wil be for our posterities to refuse the popes jurisdiction (if ever motion should be made in parliament, for the reducing of that man of sinne, as God forbidde there shoulde) seeing you have not thought it unlawful to retain their Ll. and superiority, who have no better warrant for their calling then the pope might have for his, beeing confirmed by the free consent of the state. I go forward.

Thirdly, if Church government be an humane constitution, then it may be lawfull for a church governour, vz. a bishopp, archdeacon, or some other of that order, to preache, administer the sacramentes, oversee, excommunicate, &c. and to be a king. For the holy Ghoste maketh it lawful, 1. Pet. 2. 13. for any, supplying the place of an humane constitution, lawfully to be a king. And I woulde our bishopps durst denie it? Where then learne they that divinitie, that it is more against the word, for a bishop to be *Basileus*, a king, *Hyperichon*, a superiour, *Hegemon*, a captaine or governour, being titles (1. Pet. 2. 13.) sanctified by the holy Ghoste for civill officers, then *Curios*, a Lord, *Hyperpheron*, a prelate, *Euergetes*, a lords grace. The former and latter, vz. *Curios* and *Euergetes*, being denied by our Saviour Christe (Luk. 22. 25.) unto bishopps or ministers, the 2. vz. *Hyperpheron*, never red in the word, for ought that I can remember. If they saye, that the abuse of Lordlines, and graceles grace is forbidden by Christe, they have bene answered, they are aunswered, and let them replye when they can; that our Saviour Christ never alowed abuse or tyrannie in civill governors, when as he doth not forbid them to rule as Lordes, or to be called grace; and therefore speaketh in this place, Luk. 22. 25. of the lawful and sanctified use of civil governement, and titles, which sanctified use being lawful in the civil magistrates, he denieth to be lawful in his ministers. He denieth, I saye, the use both of the name and title of the magistracie, and also of the office unto his ministers. Because it were palpable absurd, to thinke that the Lord in deed forbiddeth his ministers to beare the name and title of the magistrats, whereas he granteth them the office and dignitie, whereunto that name or title may be lawfully joyned in the civil magistrate. Here I knowe that the example of Ely the high priestes civill government, will be brought in for the confirmation of the civil authoritie of our bishops, whereunto I wil make no other answer at this time, but that I hope that our bishops do not thinke, that we under her Majesties raign and peaceable government, are brought to that exigencie, which the prophet threatneth should come upon the people of Judah (Isa. 3. 6): namely, that we shoulde take holde of some bishop, and saye, thou shalt be our governour, because we meane that our fall and overthrow shalbe under thine hand. For when Ely joyned the civil goverment of the Jewes with his priesthood, then the philistims gave the Jewes a shameful overthrow, and tooke away the Arke of God. So that unlesse we holde it lawful for us to seeke such meanes, as wherby we shal be sure to fal before our enemies, and to be bereaved of the Arke of God; I see not why the example of Ely (who to make the best of it, sheweth some extraordinarye thing proper unto Ely, and not to bee drawen into example by others) should make it lawful for ministers to beare civil offices. For in deed it sheweth nothing els for our instruction, but that a readie way to bring a final destruction upon the land, is, for the parliament to give our ministers leave to joyn the magistracie and the ministery together. And here it woulde be knowne, whether they (whoe in their bookes have whotly and egerly pursued this example of Ely, to defend the civill jurisdiction of ministers) have not therein some secret meaning, if opportunitie woulde serve, to aspire unto the crowne. For they may be suspected to hope, if ever an *interregium* should fall (as I trust in God it shall never be in their dayes) that the estate would think it most convenient, to commit the soveraigntie unto som conscionable Churchman, untill it may be otherwise disposed off. And therefore it may be justly suspected, that in disputing from the example of Ely, they had one eye unto this wherof I speak. For they may proove far better by the example of Ely, who was the chiefe magistrate in his dayes, that a minister may joyne a whol kingdome unto his ministerie, rather then any other inferiour office.

To conclude this point. Seeing, First to make that which belongeth to the outwarde worship of God, to have no more ground out of the worde, then that which appertaineth unto the civil magistracie. Secondly, to allowe of the popes superioritie as lawful. And thirdly, to holde that a minister may be both a king and a minister, are wicked and absurd assertions, and as we see directly against the word. Therefore it is wicked in like maner, to make the ecclesiastical goverment to be an humane constitution : and not unlikely by little and little, to pave the way for the undermining of the civil governement; as the reasons which our Bb. do bring for the maintenaunce of their superioritie, and experience under poperie do give us just cause to suspect. For why may not a forged donation of Constantine, or Lodovicus pius, in time joyne the crowne of England, to the sea of Davids or Bangor especially ; whiche from Joseph of Aramathea, can be prooved to have a little better continuance of personall succession, then Rome can from Peter ; as well, as it joyned the kingdome of Sicilia, the Dukedome of Naples, the Ilandes, Corsica, Sardinia, &c : unto the popes Miter.

The thirde reason is thus framed, and I will be

briefe. That forme of Church governement, and that booke or bookes, which teacheth, that there is something to be observed, besides that, which was included in the commission given by our saviour Christ unto his Apostles (Math. 28. 19) wherin they were enjoyned to teache men, to observe whatsoever he commanded, is a governement execrable and accursed by the spirite of God in plaine wordes, Gal. 1. 9.: and so are the bookes. And being such, far be it, that eyther the goverment, or the books shoulde be maintained by the authoritie of this high court of parliament. Such a curse being pronounced against the maintaining of execrable things, as we finde Deuter. 7. 15. But our forme of church governement in Wales, and this booke with many others, published by authoritie teache the same. For where is it included, muchlesse prescribed in the word, that our Saviour Christ abolished an outward government of the Church in the Levitical pollicy, being in no sort an humane ordinance, but altogether prescribed by the lord himselfe, to the end, that under the Gospel there should be no governement of the Church but an humane ordinance, that might lawfully be changed at the pleasure of man? Or where is it revealed, that the Apostles gave the civill magistrate, when any should be in the Churche; the commission to abolishe the Presbytery by them established; because there was no christian magistrate in the Churche, as our adversaries themselves confesse:

but as the worde sayth,* established by the Lorde; and therefore not to be abrogated by the magistrate, untill his pleasure in that poynte be farther knowne: therefore this government, and this book or books, are execrable and accursed.

Lastly, that forme of Church governement, and that booke or books, which affirme the kingdom of Christe in the outwarde governement, to be a kingdome that cann be shaken, that is, altered, or remooved as the ceremoniall governement was: affirme that, which is contrarye to the expresse written word of God. Heb. 12. 28. and therfore are not to be tollerated. But our Church government in Wales by L.Bb. archdea. dumb ministers, commiss. &c, in their making of ministers, excommunication, &c: is such, and suche is this unlearned heape and sophisticall booke, with the rest written on this argument. And therefore both the booke or bookes, affirme things contrarie to the worde, and so are not be tollerated, unlesse we would have the Lorde to bring speedie shame and confusion uppon us, for mayntaining sinne by lawe.

The proposition is apparant. Because that by the word kingdome that cannot be shaken in the afoersaid place (Heb. 12. 28.) must needs be ment perticularly (whatsoever signification els thei have as more generall) the outward government established under the Gospel,

* 1 Cor. 13. 5. 11; Ephe. 4. 4; Rom. 12. 6; 1 Pet. 4. 10; Math. 21. 25.

since the abolishing of the ceremoniall lawe, which being compared, in regard of continuance, and removing or doing awaie with Moses his government, (is saide to be a kingdome that cannot be shaken) that is, such as the Lorde never meaneth to alter again unto the worlds end : as to have any other government placed in stead thereof by himselfe, much lesse by man, whereas that under Moses is affirmed by the prophet Haggaie (2. 7.), and heare by the apostle, to be a kingdom or government that could be shaken, that is, altered. And this is the proper meaning of the place, Heb. 12. 28. For by the kingdome that cannot be shaken, must needes be meant, either the assurance of salvation, which we have under the Gospel, or our injoying and professing of externall life, or else the outwarde governement, not only in the preaching of the word, and administration of the sacraments, but in the Church officers, the manner of their choise and their subjects, wherin they are to be occupied. But as concerning assurance of salvation in this life, and the profession of eternal life in heaven, which the fathers enjoyed under the lawe, it was no more to be shaken then ours, the meanes thereunto by the word preached, they want no more then we doe. And so in these respectes they had a kingdome that could no more be shaken then ours. It remaineth therefore, that theirs was to be shaken, in regarde to their outward government which was abolished by the comming of Christ. And therefore ours immooveable in this respect, until his second comming, which were senslesse to be affirmed if Christ in his kingdome, whereunto we are subject, had instituted no externall regiment of his Churche. Can that be unmooveable which is not at all? More senseles it were to think, this kingdom to be immutual in regard of the sacraments, and not of the persons, and officers, who are to deale with those misteries.

To come againe unto you of this honourable court of Parliament, you are not to learne, that to defend, by lawe, or to countenance by authoritie, the breach of gods ordinance is the defence of sin, and that the defence of sinne, is the hatred of God, who rewardeth them to their faces that hate him, Deut. 7. 10. and therefore also you are not to be taught, what horrible sinnes you shall commit, if hereafter you stil maintaine such plain and manifest impieties (Numb. 26. 9.) They are no trifles as you see. For I assure you, that Dathan and Abiram the sonnes of Eliab, men famous in the congregation had more colour of right, to claime unto themselves either the civill governement from Moses, or the priesthood from Aharon. Because they were the sonnes of Reuben the first borne, (unto whose lotte, had he not defiled his fathers bedd (Gen. 49. 4.), by all likelihood, either the scepter or the priesthood should have fallen) then these usurpers have to claim the places they are in, whereunto either by right of inheritance according to the flesh, or ordinaunce from God, they came by no title.

Here it must needes followe (you of this honorable assemblie having regarde unto the estate of your soules and bodies before the Lord, and your good names among posterities) that if these things set downe be true (if not bring uppon me deserved shame and punishment) you wil either labor to redres the miserable estate of distressed wales, by erecting there a godly ministerie, and abolishing all Cananitishe relikes, or for the defence of a fewe unconscionable and godlesse men, adventure to undergoe the fierie and flaming execution, of the burning decree of Gods wrath : My Lords, and you the rest of this assemblie, be not deceived, the Lord of heaven is angrie with you and his whole hoast for the Babilonish garments of these Achanes. (Joh. 7. 9. 21.) Retayne them no longer if you would not fall before the enemie. When the L. shall plead with you, your wives, children, family, and the whole land, with pestilence or with blood, (Ezek. 38. 22) as he is likely to do for these wedges of execrable golde, it is not the pontificall Lordships of Bishops, at whose commaundement the Lords sword wil returne again into his sheath, when your gasping soules shal cry for mercy at the Lords hand ; it is not the proud and popelike Lordshipps of Bishopps, their usurped jurisdictions, their profane excommunications, their pitiles murthering of soules, their railinge slaunders against Gods truth and his servants, their impious brething of the holy Ghost upon their Idol priestes, that wil drive the Lord to give you any comfort. Let me therfore (thogh my person be base) entreat you, that the judgements of God against sin, both in this life, and in that other of eternal wo and misery may apeare so terible in your eies, and of that undoubted consequence, as you wil no longer retain under your government those things, whose continuance do give the Lord just cause in this life to pronounce this sentence by the mouth of Jeremie against everie on of you, (Jere. 22. 29) that wil not promote this sute, and execute the same. O earth, earth, earth, here the wordes of Jehovah, write these men destitute of children, men that shall not prosper in their dayes, yea there shal not bee a man of their seed that shall prosper, and bee a parliament man, or beare rule in England any more. And in the life to come to say moreover: These mine enemies that would not have me to beare rule (Luk. 19. 27.), by mine owne lawes over them and their people, bring hither and slay before my face, yea bind them hand and foote, and throw them to utter darknes, there is weeping and gnashing of teth. And let me, craving upon my knees, with all submission and earnestnes, and more earnest if it were possible to obtane, that my countrymen by your meanes may have the word preached, even the meanes whereby they may live for ever, with

Abraham, Isaac, and Jacob, in the kingdome of heaven. Graunt them this, my Lordes, though I dye for it. And this the Lord knoweth is the only scope of my writing, and not the discrediting or galling of our Lorde Bb. Let not their places withstand the salvation of my brethren, and the true service of God among them, and if ever I either write or speake more against them, any further then their places are like to be the ruine of hir Majestie and the whole state, let it cost me my life. Here me in this sute, good my Ll. The reward thereof your soules shall find; otherwise I am likelie to become a wearisom and an importunate sutor unto this high assemblye. The cause is so juste, that if it were, as sometimes it was, by the apostle him selfe decided in the Athenianes Areopago, a court for heathen justice of famous and celebrated memory, I doubt not but it should be hard. And shal it not have justice in the christian parliament of England? Justice, my Lords, I say; for I seeke nothing else, but that the statutes of the God of judgment and justice may be made known in my country, wher now they are unhard of. Then the which I know not what can be more just; neither can I see what justice in truth can be administred by them that neglect this cause. Trulie for mine owne parte, God aiding me, I wil never leave the suite; though there shoulde bee a thousand parliaments in my dayes, untill I either obtaine it at your handes, or bring the Lord in vengeance and bloud to plead against you, for repelling his cause. I hope it wil not be here said, that the parliament can doe nothing in the matter, because hytherto all Churche causes have bin referred unto the convocation house and the leaders thereof, namelie to our Bishops. And doe you meane it shalbe so still? Then shall you still maintain these horrible profanations of Gods sanctuarie, whereof I have spoken. Then may it be said unto your shame, that Sion lying uppon the ground, and mourning like a widow, stretched out her handes unto the parliament of England, but could find no comfort. Then may you stil be said to betray Gods truth, to betray the salvation of his people, yea and to betray the liberties of this parliament. For what assembly is there in the land, that dare chaleng unto it selfe the ordering of religion, if the parliament may not? When you say, then, that you may not deale in the matters of religion, because the determinations of that cause is referred unto the Bishops assembled in the convocation house, who in their Cannons, are to provide and see that the church be not in a decaied state, do you not thereby thinke you rob your selves of your owne prerogative and liberties, and take order that the church without controversie may be starved and spoiled?

In deed if the convocation house were such as it ought to be, vz. a sinod of sincere, and godly learned ministers, wherein matters of relligion were determined of according to the worde, and the cause of God heard with out partiallitie, then in deed were it their partes to set downe for the direction of the parliament, such thinges as were behoofull for the glorie of God, and the good of his church, and the parliament by their direction according to the word, ought to enjoine all the ministers and people, whatsoever should be thus enacted by the civil state. And if the convocation house were such an assembly, then were it not laweful for the parliament, to establish any thing in the matters apertaininge unto the pure worship of God, among their people, but that wherein they shoulde be directed, by the advise of the churche governours. For as in a christian common wealth, where the civill state sincerely favoureth the true worship of the Lord, it is not tollerable, no not for the right and lawful, muchlesse (say the usurping tiranical governors of the church) establish any thing in the church, but by the authoritie of the christian magistrat: so wher there are godly, wise and sincere ministers, it is unlawfull for the civill governour, to order any thing in the church within his dominions, but by their direction according to the word. So that I doe not denie, but that the convocation house being an assembly of true and lawful church officers, you ought to use their advise and direction how the wants of the church might be supplied. But you shoulde not permit them to enact what they would by their owne authoritie, especially their decrees being now as they are, to the ratifying of corruptions, and to the continuance of ungodly callings within these dominions. And if you mean to give over your right in dealing with the case of God unto the convocation house, to what end shall the states of the land meete together in parliament, be ever againe sued unto.

But, alasse! that any thing in church causes, shalbe referred unto that assemblie, which would not stand as it doth, if there weare that good order in the church which the Lord requireth, and as long as it doeth stand, must needs be the cause of all disorders therein, and must needs be a meanes of continuing that starving ignoraunce which raigneth in this land. Why my Lords, to referre the cause of religion unto the Convocation house, is nothing els, but to charge the wolves under paine of the displeasure of careful shepherds, to see that the lambes may be fedd, besides the injurious derogation that thereby is offered unto the liberties of this house.

And that it may appear how justly I apeal from that sinagogue, unto this high court of parliament, and what small hope there is to be conceived of reforming the abuses of our Church, if the redresse be committed unto that meeting; you of the honorable court of parliament are to understand, that the convocation house condemneth this cause of Christ now in hand, before it be hard: and that their onely endevours who are there mett, is howe to prevent him from bearing rule in the Church by his owne lawes. For it is well knowne, that all of them have banded and linked them selves together, to maintaine the corruptions of our Church, whereof I have before spoken; as the ungodly and popish hierarchie of bishops, the ignorant ministery, &c. Which thing shal be manifested by the consideration of the persones, who are admitted unto the consultation and meeting. And they are of 2. sorts. First, these whoe by reason of the superiority they usurp over their brethren, must needs be the chief doers in that house, how ignorant, unconscionable, and unfit for the government of the Church soever they be. Of which number, are our Archbb. and L.bishops, &c. The second sort is of these, who having no interest to be there, in respect of anye superioritie they beare in the Churche, are therefore elected and chosen to be there as the clarks of the Convocation house, &c. But there is such freedome and liberty in the choyse of these men, that great care and heede is alwayes had by our L.Bb. that none shalbe chosen thither, but such, as for good causes are knowen to bee utter enemies unto all sinceritie, and strong maintainers of the established corruptions: if any other by some meanes be gotten thither, who doth but once mention the healing of the wounds of our Church, he is straightwaies taken for a Nicodemus among them; namely, for a man favoring that side, which none of the great Scribes and Pharises can brook, and lightly they take that order with him, which the Jewes tooke with those, who professed our Saviour Christ; that is, they bannish him out of their Synagogue. To be briefe, whosoever are of the house there is nothing done there, but what the former sort; to wit, L.archb. and Bb. would have enacted. For the rest, eyther cannot or wil not withstand their proceedings. The whole sway then, and direction of this synod, being in their hands, who are for the most part, the greatest cause of the teares of our Church; will you referre the ordering of religion, and the reformation of the church unto the Convocation house? I have alreadye shewed, that you ought to be so far from permitting unto L.Bb. the disposition of any thing behofull unto the Church of God, as the very names and places should be razed from under your government. And wofull experience these 30. full yeares, hath taught us what a lamentable reformation these men now bring to passe, if they may have their owne wils. Why these men, my Lords, and consequently, the whole Convocation house are in judgement contrarye unto our Saviour Christ; (Luk. 22. 25.) for they holde it lawfull for ministers to be Lordes over their brethren. These men, my Ll., are of judgement, that the exhortation of the Apostle Peter was not directed unto them? The Elders which are among you, sayth the Apostle, I beseech, which am also an Elder, and a witnes of the sufferings of Christ, and also a pertaker of the glorye that shalbe revealed, Feede the flocke of God which dependeth uppon you, caring for it, not by constraint, but willingly; not for filthy lukers sake, but of a readie minde; not as though ye were Lords over Gods heritage, but that ye may be ensamples to the flocke; and when the chiefe shepheard shall appeare, you shall receive an incorruptible crowne of glory. These men I say, are in judgement, contrary unto this blessed Apostle, for they thinke it lawful for them to be Lords over Gods heritage. They are of judgment, that Christ Jesus was not so faythfull as Moses, in the goverment of his owne house. And do you then thinke that they care how unfaythfull they doe behave themselves in the oversight of the Church? They hold the government of the Church to be an humane ordinaunce, and so holde the Pope to have sufficient warrant of his hierarchie. They, my Ll., hold the kingdome of Christe in the outward government, to be a kingdome, the lawes whereof, may be chaunged and abrogated, at the pleasure of man. They do not stick to affirme it lawful for them to teach many thinges not included in the commission given by our saviour Christ unto his Apostles. These men reject as untrue, that which the spirite of God hath set downe by the Apostle Paule, 1. Cor. 1. 21. Rom. 10. 14. which is, that men are ordinarilye saved by the preaching of the word. For they are perswaded that salvation may be ordinarily attayned unto by reading; and so they are perswaded, that the Lorde hath promised his spirit to seale that doctrin in the hearts of men (Ephes. 1. 13.), which through preaching was never made knowen unto them. What care then will they have, to see the people provided for of preching, wheras they are not perswaded of the ordinary necessitie thereof? They, my Ll., maintaine the continuance of the dumb and ignorant ministery, whereby our Church hath long since gotten her bane. Their judgement is, that they may be tollerated for lawful ministers, in a christian commonwelth, and that the parliament may securely maintain them in our Churche, without all feare of Gods judgementes for tollerating them! O the great hand of God in punnishing our ingratitude, that in this cleare light of the gospell, they who take upon them to be Archseers, willingly see not, that none can be lawfull embassadors of Jesus Christ, but they out of whose mouthes this embassage is heard; *We beseech you in Christs steed, that you be reconciled unto God* (3. Cor. 5.) : And yet such is the blindnes of the convocation house, that they cannot see this.

But I blush to thinke, that they dare once presume to give any countenance unto nonresidencie, that gastly and fearfull sinne: and yet behold notwithstanding, they are not onely all of them guiltie thereof themselves, but even in the books which they have published unto the world, in the defence of their corruptions, they have not bene ashamed to advouch the lawfulnes of this unnaturall and desperat murther: yea the verye pulpits have rung again and againe, with invectives against al those that withstood this their madnes. O, my Ll. and you the rest of the R. honourable and worshipful of this high court of parliament, I can not stay my selfe, but I must needes in this place, crie unto you for helpe and justice, against these unnaturall men. The Convocation house, my Ll., defendeth nonresidencie to be lawfull! Nonresidencie, my Ll., is defended to bee lawfull in the Convocation house! And will you then trust them with the oversight of the people, who are of judgment, that they may lawfully starve and murther them? Can you hope for any good to come unto the church of God from that councel, where it is enacted, that it may be lawfull for a bond of murthering nonresidents to destroy the same? If therfore in the parliament of Englande, there be any care of the glorye of God, and the libertie of his Church; if any pitie and compassion of the starved soules of men, let others bee trusted to provide foode for your people, and not those, whose very judgements are so darkened, that they hold it allowable by the worde for them to take order that men may not be fedd. It is now meet, my Ll., that they who holde it lawfull for men to make a trade of murther, should be allowed for physicions. And what els are they, who defende the lawfulnes of nonresidencie, but suche as professe it lawfull for men to bee maintayned (rather then they shoulde want living) even by the murthering of their brethren?

Is it not great pitie then, but that this Convocation house should be stil countenanced by the state, to be the only place whence reformation of all the things out of order in our Church should be expected? For therein doubtles, any thing shal be heard, which may tende to the furtherance of the gospell; seeing none sound (few excepted) are admitted into that assembly, who are not guiltie of the merciles and cruell murther of soules, as beeing all of them for the most part, cursed and bloody nonresidents. And is it not great pitie, but that the parliament should staye and go no further in the reformation of religion, then it should bee directed by the Convocation house. For it may be hoped, out of question, that the Convocation house will see, that no calling be henceforth tollerated in the ministerie, but such as the Lord in his worde warranteth to be lawfull. And therefore it may bee hoped, that the leaders thereof will not sticke to put downe Archbishops, and L.Bb. that Christ alone, by the officers which he in his word hath appointed may rule in his church. They will not abide that anye blemished and maymed Levit should come neere to the Lords Sanctuarie, nor any pharasaicall high priest shoulde usurpe anye authoritie over his brethren in this lande. If this hope might be conceived of them, then in deed

woulde they bee meete to cure the diseases of our
church. But the truth is, that there is no reason why
this should be expected at their hands, because they
are so far (as this whole land knoweth) from having
anye remorse of the unlawfull and ungodly callings
wherein they nowe remaine, that their practises against
God and his trueth, doe proclaime unto the worlde,
that they never meane to restore againe her owne
authoritie unto the Churche, whereof by their Lordships it hath bene spoyled.

I have determined with my selfe, not to trouble this
honorable assemblie at this time, with any large dis-
course concerning these men and their dealings:
otherwise, I would shew by evident profs, that they
(and so the whole Convocation house) are guiltie of
such crimes, as the favorablest interpreter of their proceedings, woulde of necessitie be drawne to give this
sentence against them, namely; That they are intollerable oppugners of Gods glory, and utter enemies
unto the liberties of his Church. And they should
also be drawne to confesse, that the parliament in
maintayning the Convocation house, did maintayn and
defend, together with the hindering and smoothering
of the trueth, not only the deformed ruines; but also
the lamentable oppression of the Church. So that it
should appeare, that as long as that house standeth,
as at this day it doth, there could be no hope at all,
that either Gods heavenly trueth should have free

passage, or the Churche her lybertie in this kingdome. The briefe heades of the publike crimes, whereof the leaders of the Convocation house are guiltie, I will here set downe, and they shalbe hereafter evidently prooved, if they unto whose charge they are laid dare deny them.

First, therefore, their very callings and places, that is, the callings and places of our Archbishops and L.Bb. are such as they cannot possibly but dishonour God, and bereave the Church of her libertie by continuing in them. Secondly their practises in those places, for the maintenaunce of their tyrannicall superioritie, and others the corruptions of the Church, which they wilfully, contrary unto all trueth and æquitie, doe maintaine, are such as by them they have not onely monstrously maymed the outward face of the church, in the matter of governement and ceremonies, but also grievously wounded the same, in the matters of doctrine and sacramentes: unto the mayntenance of all which corruptions in the government of the Churche, in the ceremonies, in the doctrin and sacraments, they have joyned the crimes of seducing and deceiving the civill state and people, by bearing all estates in hand, that al hath bene and is well in the Church; and in like manner, as much as in them lay, they have vexed and persecuted as many of the deare servants of God, as have but entended to motion the redresse of any of the former corruptions. Hereof if I shall not be able to proove the eyes and leaders of this synagogue, and consequently the whol house to bee guiltie; let mee, to the terror of all slaunderers, be put to all the torments that may bee invented. The Convocation house cannot here object, that I deal injuriously with the whol assembly, by laying unto the charge of the whol, those crimes whereof our Bb. alone are guiltie. For the whole house, never as yet, disavowed the hierarchie of Bb., their practises in urging subscription, in maintayning the dumbe ministerie, nonresidencie, &c. And untill the corruptions of the Bb. be overthrown in that assembly, the whol house shall be still justly subject unto the former accusations.

See now, my Lords, whether they doe not bewray their impietie who think, that men weary them selves about small matters, when they call for a reformation of the church. And see whether there be not many and urgent causes, to inforce the parliament to take the government of the Church out of the hands of these men, unlesse the continuance of the ruinous breaches of our Church would be stil maintained. It is not the matter of capp, surplice, tippet, and other beggerlie and popish ceremonies, whence al the dissention and dissagreement in our church is sprong up. But the controversies arise, because our Archbb. and Bb. are not permitted with the silence and consent of the servants of God, to smother, persecute, deprave and corrupt the truth of that true religion which in name they professe, and to undermine and captivate the church of God in this land. Those who withstand their ungodly proceedings, have hitherto dutifully kept them selves within the bonds of the calings wherin the Lord hath placed them; they have in al submission and duty entreated that the cause of God might be equally hard, and that her Majestie and the parlament would amend the things proved to be amis, they have never as yet, presumed themselves, to take in hand the correction of any thing. But how quietly on the other side, have the leaders of the convocation house behaved them selves, when a redres hath bin caled for at the hands of the civil state? Surely they have alwais hitherto presently betaken themselves, to imprisonments and bonds and would never suffer the truth to have the hering, nor any man with quietnes to stand in the defence therof. And therefore also, al the tumults that hereafer are like to arise in the Church of God within this land, about these controversies, the leders of the convocation house, are the causes thereof, for they wil not yeeld unto the truth, but labour by all meanes possible, to smother the same. Gods servants cannot winke at their proceedings, unlesse they would betray Gods truth, and the libertie of his church. The least parte of the sinnes of our Bb. hath bin in the maintenance of unprofitable, superstitious, and corrupt ceremonies. If they would but yeeld free passage unto the truth, and hir authority unto the church in other matters, they should not be gretly molested for these things. And woe be unto them, if they had rather provoke god and his church to battel against them for the defence of the truth, then receive the light, and grant peace unto the church. Concerning her Majestie, who (as it is thought) can never be induced to aulter the established government, I answere, that if it be made known unto her, and proved out of the word that the established regiment of the church is traiterous against the Majestie of Jesus Christ, that it confirmeth the popes supremacie. O therfore it is dangerous unto her crown, that it is besides the commission given by our Saviour Christ unto his apostles; and therefore accursed, that it sheweth them to be void of all care of religion, who wittingly countenance the same, and that it calleth for the judgments of God against her, and her kingdom, and then if shee yeeld not unto the razing of all sinful callings out of the church, I will not desire to live, if this be thought a matter worthy of death, for a man to be dutyfully perswaded of his soveraigne. Be it that her Majestie hath bin moved, by some of this house, for the redresse of the church, you should move her againe, and againe, and never leave until you be heard. Great matters are never brought to passe, without great and mighty endevours. Our sinnes have otherwise deserved, then, that the Lord should at the first encline mercy unto us, in the sight of her highnes.

Would any of you alter any part of the government of his family, being perswaded by leud flatterers, that all were well, unlesse the abuse were shewed, and you earnestly dealt with for a reformation. And can you then marvel, that our soveraigne is hardly drawne to reforme the church, whose estate in her hearing, is daily said out of the pulpit to be most florishing, wheras the deformity therof is not made knowne unto her. I know it is no smal persuasion that should drive a monarch to abrogat the receved constitutions, and establish new, unles the unanswerable necessity thereof were made knowne unto her or him. I am perswaded that her Majestie knoweth not the exacting necessitie that lieth uppon her sholders of reforming the church. Shee knoweth not the estate of her untaught and damned subjects to be as it is. Wherefore serve parliament men, if her eies must be in al places to see every thing, and what doe you see, if you do not see our miserie and lament it? I grant indeed, that of this point she ought to be most careful, but if of oversight, the waightiest matters be omitted, shoulde not you put her in mind hereof? And in submission entreat her, and never leave entreating, untill shee yeeld to turne away the wrath of God from her and her kingdome, by abollishing ungodly ordinances, and restoring beauty unto Zion.

Well, I have forged the most notable slanders that ever were coined, or els, the state of my cuntrey under her Majesties government is very miserable, and yours no lesse lamentable, if it so continue. And if you make not the same knowne unto her Majestie, and see it be speedely amended, the Lord make Quene Elizabeth, and her crown free, from the bloude of her destroyed people. And I pray God if it be his will, that their soules be not required at your hands in the day wherein quick and dead shalbe judged.

But it may be, that you wil pretend the waute to be so difficult that it cannot possiblie be performed. Do what lieth in you, and then the Lord is answered. The farther you go herein, the esier wilbe the passage, you are desired no more, then not to countenance sinn, and for reformation to go no farther then meanes will reach. Because it is a worke of difficultie, therefore must you needs hinder the same by lawe as you doe, by tollerating these abuses; Because the whol worke is difficult, therefore shal it not begin; Because it is a hard matter to plant the ordinance of God, therefore must the breache thereof be in force, and maintained? Because in Canaan the sonnes of Anak (Num. 13. 14.), and towns walled up to heaven (mountains of pretensed excuses, have ben seene) therefore must you needs suffer the people, brought by her Majestie and you, out of Egipt, to remaine stil in the wildernes, on this side Jordan, even under these men, the dumb ministers, L.Bb. I meane, which are fit for nothing els, then to be leaders, whensoever oportunitie shall serve, to bring the people again into Egipt? (Num. 14. 4.) Because our land, by reason of our continuance in sinn, and that wee have not had skilful workmen among us, doth not now bring forth religion and godlinesse in the measure it should, therefore must you needs be sure, that profanesse and atheisme shalbe sowen, and the breach of Gods lawe flourish there, in the persons of those men? (Ezek. 23.) Therefore the just Lord wil be just in the midst of you, whensoever he reckoneth for these things, because you are so far from doing what you may in the planting of godlinesse, that you suffer impietie against his Majestie to bear sway, and that by law and authority.

Concerning the hardnesse of the work, this I make knowne unto you, that if you wilbe ruled by the cannon of the word, you shalbe able with ease and the good liking of your people, to do so much therein, as you shal deliver your owne lives from the wrath of God. But if that rule shal take place no farther, then it may stand with the continuance of Lord Bishops, and other corruptions of the ecclesiasticall state, I see not what you can say unto the Lord, when he hath made you an astonishment, and an hissing unto all the nations under heaven: but surely thou art just in all that is come upon us, for wee would not be ruled by thy words (Nehe. 9. 39.)

Wel, the word teacheth and requireth of you 2. things and no more, in this worke. In both it requireth your practise, if you would be directed by it. First it requireth, that Wales may be redressed by proclaiming that commission given by our Saviour Christ unto his apostles, Math. 28. 19. 20., in every corner thereof, and both the parts of the commission, it requireth to be kept inviolably ; as well that, of goe preach and baptise, as the other, of teach them to observe, whatsoever I have commanded you. Secondly, while you stay the Lords leasure to raise up fit men for this worke in every congregation, it requireth, that the people where preachers cannot be placed at the first, may have som stay, that inconveniences be avoided. For the Lord will not have religion, so undiscretly established, as that the inconveniences that might growe thereby unto the civil state, as much as may be, be not wisely prevented ; in the effectinge hereof, 2. things are to be looked unto, both of them greatlie furthering the worke. First the blessing of God is to be labored for, by humbling your selves and your people with Daniel before the Lord (Dan. 9. 1. 3.), in fasting and praier, and then you shal see he wilbe with your endevours. Secondly you must enjoine every one according unto his place, to have a hand in this worke, and encourage the gentlemen, and people that shalbe found forward, by gracing and countenancing them for their forwardnesse in religion, and shewing that the more forward they be, the more credit they are like to purchase with your Hh.

(Nom. 14. 39.) And you must not suffer an uncircumcised mouth to bring a slander upon that good land, whereunto the Lord offereth to bring you and your people, if you would obey (Nom. 14. 10.), much lesse, to lift up a stonn against Caleb or Joshuah, that withstand the fury of a whol wicked hoast in the defence of the Lord. For otherwise, if you suffer al to sit stil, and looke uppon our desolations, the most to live on the sweetnes of our ruines, and discountenance all that labour therein, you can looke for nothing else shortly; but that lamentable complaint, and it is a great work of God, that we have heard the same long agoe, of everie possessor in this land. Whyther shall wee goe? Our brethren and their hard intertainment have discouraged our harts (Deut. 1. 18.); woulde to God that we had died in the Land of Egipt, would to God we weare dead: were it not better for us to turne into Egipt? com let us make a captaine and returne thyther (Nom. 14. 3.) The land in deed is a good land, whereunto, when our soveraigne brought us out of Egipt, wee entended to make our jorney: but, alasse! we are never able to stand against the povertie, losses, imprisonment, discountenance by our superiors, that our brethren have sustained, which have set their faces against this land, never able to swallowe up the slanders and bitter names of Puritans, precisians, traitos, seditious libellers, &c. that we see raised against those that would bring us thyther. And therefore, my Ll.

and the rest of the high assemblie, in vaine shall you use other meanes, and leave this unattempted.

The redresse of Wales consisteth of 2. partes, both must be speedely set upon by your Hh., or els certainly the judgements of God will finde you out. First you must abolishe out of the Churche whatsoever you shal finde to be a breach of gods ordinance (as I have prooved dumbe ministers, nonresidents, and L.Bb. to be) or els your reformation will be little better then that of the Samaritanes (2. Kin. 17. 33.), who feared Jehovah, but worshipped their owne gods. I woulde have it marked in this place, what is required at the handes of the parliament, that it may thereby appeare, whether with any colour of reason, this part of the petition in hand can be denied. The parliament is desired to enact, that no unlawfull calling be tollerated under the government within the church of God in Wales; if they will not yeeld unto this part of the suite, now put up in the behalfe of that people; what cloake doe they leave unto themselves, whereby they may but cover their small care to glorifie God? Is not the case to be astonied at, that an assembly professing true religion, cannot be drawne to yeeld unto so just a request, it is a hard matter I grant, to build the church of God: Men most willing to bring that worke to passe, cannot doe it; but there is no difficultie in the worlde for the parliament of England to manifest that, although they cannot go so far in promoting the

Gospell as they woulde wishe; yet that they will not at any hand maintaine by lawe any thing which may hinder the course thereof. Wel, let as manye as are parliament men looke unto this, as sure as the Lord liveth, they shall answere one day, before him, who is the judge of quicke and dead, and give a reason why they would not consent to root out sinne, and the breach of gods law, out of this common wealth. Do they seek the innovation of the state, who desire, that no lawe or statute may be in force, which upholdeth the transgressing of Gods holy institution? Or may they be accounted dangerous subjects unto their prince, who cannot abide that any treson against God should be countenanced? Wel, this branche of the suite is such, as the Tridentine conspiracie would blush to profes the rejecting therof. What then may be thought of the high court of parliament, if it cannot be there granted?

The second meanes for you to redress the estate of Wales must bee this; you must place as many godly learned men as can be found, to call the people, and see them provided for. But here great advice is to be taken, where, and howe they be placed. First then, you are to looke out the places that are fittest, by all likelihood, to receive the word, and unto those, to have the speciallist regard. For seeing you are not able, at once, to furnish the whole countrie with able men, you must first have regard of that part of

the harvest which is most readie for the mowers.
This respect we see the spirite of God to have had,
Act 16. 7. Where the spirit would not suffer Paule to
go to Bythnia, but rather tooke his journey to Macedonia, where, by revelation, verse 9. 10, hee was
assured that there was preparation made for the receiving of the gospell. Concerning the other point,
the ministers that shall be sent must not be scattered
a sunder one here, and another there in the countrie;
neither sent one by one, but many must be sent together, and placed so nere one another as may be. And
so the ministers, having ædification, and comfort one
by another, shall neither decay in their gifts, nor be
discouraged; and the people, by this means, shall be
sure to be thorowly called. If the complaint be made
for want of sufficient men, and sufficient stay for their
living: For the men, take all those whome the Lorde
hath made fit for this worke, and he can require no
more at your hands, until he raise up more, which, if
he never do, your good endevours, and encouragemnte
unto students and others, not being wanting to bring
this to passe, he cannot in justice punish you, though
your people be not taught. Because you have seen
all those well bestowed whom he quallified for the
calling, and so doe now expect a blessing from him
upon your labours, that you might send more. The
subterfuge will be but the coat of a net, to aske (as
comonly your prelats do) how there should be possibly

founde, as many learned men as Wales requireth, seeing they who are found, are not placed there. And do you deale well with the Lorde, that because all cannot be brought at once to serve him, as he willeth, therefore they that may shall not? The same is to bee said of the ministers livings. Remove the dumb ministers, non-residents, L.Bb. (if you will not do this you go besides the word of God, and so there is no direction for you) and there will be more livings void, able to maintain godly ministers, then shall be, I fear me, good men found to supply their places. And, verily, I marvail, what men perswade themselves the Lord to be; whereas they thinke he can be satisfied with such siclic shifts? Is it not a strange matter to find Church livings in Wales for L.Bb. non-residents, and dumb ministers, to sin against God, and starve soules withall, and deny any to be there for godly ministers to honor God and worke the salvation of his people. The children must starve for want of bread, because the dogs before their eies must be fed therewith. Good reason? yea, but the removing of those men would be likely to set the land on fire. Marke how subtill the devil is, in the maintenaunce of his kingdome. When godly ministers are deprived, because they will not linke themselves with wicked Bb. to betray the kingdome of Christ, and overthrow the lawes of this land, there is no inconvenience feared. But if Satan's messengers be once shoved at, behold, the land will not be able to bear this loss. I grant, indeed, that men which make no conscience for gains sake, to breake the law of the æternall, and massaker soules (as these do) are dangerous subjects, and not to be trusted any farther then they are fed.

The most of them are unsaverye salt, such as have hitherto lived upon sacriledge and the spoil of soules. Order might be taken, notwithstanding, by the magistrates, that these and their families should neyther want things necessarie for their outward estate, nor yet be maintayned in idleness. For the people, the stay for them is, eyther in regard of publike meetings on the Sabboth, or the sacraments, marriage, or buriall. For the keeping of the Sabboth, the worde requireth they should, if possiblie they can, resort where preaching is, until good ministers be placed in every parish; if the places be far, as commonly our parishes be verye large, and it is not likely in short time to plant preachers so neere together, as the people may every Sabboth resort unto them, they must be enjoyned to meete together in their parish churches, and some discreet man among themselves to read the worde, and use some forme of prayers, as shall be thought meetest, by the advise of the godly learned. Concerning the sacraments, the word requireth they should resort unto a preching minister for them, and not attempt to keep their children unbaptized any longer, then they must of necessity. Marriage is most conveniently to be done by the minister, but is no proper essential worke of the minister, and, therefore, may be solemnized by others, at the magistrates appointment. Concerning burial, it is a worke of christian charitie, and being the last duetie that we are to performe towards the departed, we ought to accompany them decently and orderly, with all comliness to the grave. The word mentioneth or includeth no forme of prayer used at buriall; therefore they are superfluous, neyther is the minister, as in an action belonging to his office, to have any more to doe herein, then any other of the brethren.

Thus I have set downe unto your Hh. the only course in regarde of substance that the worde warranteth to be taken in such a deformed estate as ours is. And nowe, my Ll. and the rest of this honorable assembly, let my counsell be acceptable unto you; breake of your sinnes, by rooting out these plants, which the Lorde never planted in his vineyarde, and your iniquities, by abandoning the same so much as in you lieth, so there might be a healing of your former oversight. If not, the Lords face will be against you, yours, and the whole land, for evil and not for good. Oh, my Lords, is it not a miserable case, that men should so live under your goverment in this life, as they cannot possibly but live in hel in the life to come? Oh, my Ll., heven cannot be obtayned when we are gon. Oh, my Ll., now is the time for the gospell to florish in Wales or never. Oh, my Ll., if her majestie and your honors (whom from my verye heart I wish the Lorde to bless) should be gone the way of all the world ; for mine owne part, the staffe of mine hope, to see any good done amongst my brethren should be broken. Blame me not, therefore, if I deal earnestly in a cause of so great a moment, and so unlikely to be obtayned of our woful posterities, whom my suit in a most neere sort concerneth. Oh, why should they have cause to say, the Lord be judge between us and the governours which were under Queene Elizabeth, in the days of our fathers, for they might have opened our eyes and healed our woundes, which, now alasse, are desperat and past recovery.

It is now full 30. yeares and upward since Babylon hath bin overthrowne in Wales, rather by the voice of her majesties good laws (whom, good Lord, forget not for this worke) then the sounde of any trumpet from the mouthes of the sonnes of Aaron among us. But alasse, what shall we and our posterities be the better for this, if Sion bee not built? And what comfort can Zerubbabel, or Nehemiah have, to bring them out of Babylon, if they meane but to reædifie Shilo, seeing it is the beautie of Sion wherein the Lorde delighteth? We have cause in deed to thanke God, that this wicked citie hath beene by her Majestie broken downe in some sort ; but are never the better, seeing the walles of

High Court of Parliament. 77

Sion lie even with the grounde. Nowe for the space of 28. yeares, no man greatly laboured to her Majestie, the parliament, or the people themselves, eyther by speaking or writing in the behalfe of eyther of these unreconcilable cities. Men belike, thinking no more to be required at their hands then the razing of Babel, and the divel as yet contenting himselfe with Bethel. The last parliament, by al liklihod the very same week upon a sodaine, the interprises of the building of both in 2. several books, issuing from 2. of the remotest corners in our lands (Southwales and Northwales) was taken in hand. The one of the books pleading the cause of Sion, and comming forth by publike authority and alowance, was directed unto her Majestie and the parliament, requiring at their hands by vertue of the lords own mandatory letters, the performance of this work, shewing by evidence of greatest antiquitye this to be required of duty at their hands, as a part of the homadge due unto his highnes, whose fœdaries and vassales all the princes and states under heaven must acknowledg them selves to be, and a portion of that inheritance being theirs by lineall dissent, from their predecessors, the godly kings and rulers, who time out minde alwaies laid their shoulders unto this burthen. The other written in weltch, (Y druch Christianogawi) printed in an obscure cave in Northwales, published by an author unknowne and more unlerned (for I think he had never read any thing but the common published resolution of R. P., a booke contayning many substantiall errors, Fryer Rush, and other shamful fables) stood to by non, and having no reason to shew why his Babilon should be rædefied, it contained it self within the hands of a fewe private men, and never durst to this houre be made knowne unto any of our magestrats. Both the books in this thing had the same successe, in that both together they fel into the hands of the prelats, who, as they pretend, are enemies unto both places, but undoubtedly unto Sion especially, as it apeared by their hard dealing with the patrone of that cause, whereas the fautors of the other, being also in their handes, were either not at al delt with, or very curteously entertained of them.* The reason of their enemity unto both, but their hatred unto Sion is, that never I feare me, meaning to go thether, and constrained by lawe to be enemies unto the other, they have of the gold of Caldea, and the drosse of Jerusalem compacted them a citty, wherewith they meane to content them selves until they returne to Babel again, or (the Lord be merciful unto them) unto a worse place. Have they not therfore good cause to be the more beholding to the on for the gold, then the other for the drosse; Wel be you assured hereof, that they who stirred up both these instruments, both at one time, will never suffer them to cease, until in Wales either a church of Christ, or a sinagogue of sathan be

* This is spoken in respect of the church government.

built. Out of question the concurring of both causes, sheweth that the lord hath som secret work in the matter. Sathans instruments for their parts, were never busier then they are at this houre, and shal I be silent? They trecherously against the lawes of God and this land seek to bring the people again unto Egipt. I according unto both, endevour never to let them rest, until it please the Lord by meanes of her Majesty and the parlament, to bring them within the land of promise, no though they were uppon Mount Nebo, whence with their eies they might view the same. They have delt, and deal secretly with poor soules in dark corners, and dare not make knowne the fabulous cause. I have delt al this while in the face of the sun, and nowe before the state of the land assembled together, I want not a good cause, and by the grace of god, it shal never want the poore defence which I cann yeld unto it, or hide the face as long as I live, whether you countenance it or no, I know that on day it shal prevail, when this wilbe the Lord knoweth best: but the matter is, whether you wil embrace Christ in the building of his Church, or Sathan in continuing the breaches thereof. Therfore entertaine this cause, and you give Sathan the foile, reject this, and you strengthen him. And try if you deny it the hearing, whether the very papists in this land, wil not be thereby encoraged to supplicate unto the parliament, that you would graunt them the liberty of their seared consciences, to commit publike idolatry.

Al that hitherto I have spoken, hath ben said either in the cause of Christ, which is a good cause, or in the behalfe of Sathan. If I seeke the building of his sinagog, wil you let me live? If of the church of Christ, wil you deny me your help? which yet againe and againe, in the name of the eternal God I require, and for the precious deth and passions sake of Jesus Christ, I earnestly desire at your handes. My Ll. and whosoever are parlament men, as you would have the Lord to entertaine your souls in the life to come, as you would have him shewe you any mercy, as you love Her Majesty and her life, as you would have the continuance of her peaceable raign over us, which the Lord undoutedly threatneth to shorten, because he woulde bring destruction upon you and us al, for the contempt of his truth, as you would not have your names razed from under heaven, as you would not have the Lord to bring upon us and our land, the Spanish, Italian, Romish or Guisian forces, as you would not have these, who shal live to see the desolation and desperat sorrow which the Lord is likely to bring upon this land, not abide to see you or your children ride, or go in the strets, as you would not have the most contemtible to stretch forth his hand upon the derest things you posses, and offer violence unto the frute of your bodies? So entertaine this cause, grant this suite, and be careful of the Lords true service in Wales. Otherwise, the vengeance of God, I feare me, will never leave you and your posterities, as long as there is a man of your houses left under heaven.

Ezekiel in deed is not nowe living, to put you in mind of the necessity of redressing the things amis, by laying open the corruptions of all estates under your government, as he doth cap. 22. of his prophesie. His words I wil set downe that you may wey our estate, with the time wherin the prophet lived, and see whether the Lorde wil spare you and us, if we stil provoke him to smite. There is a conspiracy of her prophets in the middest thereof, saith the prophet, like a roring lyon, ravening the pray, they have devoured soules, they have taken the riches and the precious thinges: they have made her many widdows in the middest thereof, her priests have broken my law, and have defiled my holy things: they have put no difference betweene the holy and profane, neither discerned between the uncleane and the cleane, and have hid their eies from my sabboth, and I am profaned among them. Her princes in the middest thereof are like wolves ravening the pray, to shed blood and to destroy soules, for their owne covetous lucre. And her prophets have daubed her with untempered morter, seeing vanities and devininge lyes unto them, saying, thus saith the Lord Jehovah, when

M

Jehovah had not spoken. The people of the land have violently oppressed, by robbing and spoiling, and have vexed the poor and needy: yea, they have opressed the stranger against right. Thus far Ezechiel. Be the sinns of our prophets, of our princes, and of our people the same, that here he speketh against, be they greater or be they lesse: yet without controversie, if the Lord may say, I have sought for a man in the parliament of England, that should make up the hedge, and stand in the gapp, before me for the land, that I should not destroy it, but I found none: then woe be unto us, for that shal follow which is set downe in the prophete. Therefore have I powred out mine indignation uppon them, and consumed them with the fier of my wrath: their own waies have I rendered upon their heads, saith the Lord Jehovah; And unlesse there were just cause to thinke that this Lorde had either already or shortly ment to pronounce this sentence against us, we might contemne and scorn at the broken assalts of the Spaniards, or any other the enemies of the Gospel, and her Majesties whosoever. But as long as we give not the right hand to the Lord, by entering into his sanctuarye, we have just cause to feare a nation that is no nation, much more a people in number as the sand which is by the seashore. Our leagues and most stable covenants with the enemies the Lord will soone disanul, standing thus at the staffes end with his Majestie, as we doe.

High Court of Parliament.

Let it not be sayd in this place, that the Lord would not have so wonderfully wrought our late deliveraunce out of the hand of the Spaniarde, if he ment at al to have called the land to reckoning for the great ignorance, and wicked ecclesiasticall constitutions, which are truly sayd to be maintained therein. For this, both Moses and Saloman, note to be the man of all those that shall not prolong their dayes (Deut. 29. 18. 49. 20.) Moses warneth al states in any case to take heed that there should not be among them man, woman, family, nor tribe, which should turne his hart away from the Lord God, so that when he heareth the wordes of the curse, he blesse him selfe in his hart, saying, I shall have peace though I walked after the stubbornenes of mine owne hart, thus adding drunkennes unto thirst. For, saith he, the Lord wil not be mercifull unto that man: but then the wrath of the Lorde shall smoke against that man, and every curse that is written in this booke shal light upon him, and the Lord shall put out his name from under heaven, and the Lord shal seperate him unto evil, according unto all the curses that is writen in the booke of the lawe. And Soloman knowing the corruptions of men to be such (Eccles. 8. 11. 13) as their harts are fully set in them to doe evil, because sentence against their evil works is not spedely executed, openly testifieth, that although a sinner doe evill an hundreth times, and the Lord prolong his days, yet it shal only be well with them that feare the Lord, and do reverence before him. But it shall not be wel with the wicked (saith he), for he shalbe like a shadow, because he feareth not before God. And therefore although at this time the Lords anger hath not visited, nor caled the sinnes of our land to account, with gret extremity by the hand of the Spanyard: yet let us be assured that it shall not goe wel with us, unlesse you of the high court of parliament shew that you feare your God, and doe reverence before him, in purging out of his holy service what soever is superfluous therein, and in adding whatsoever is wanting thereunto. The Lord by that deliverance, gave us warning that he passed by us, but so as, unlesse the corruptions of his service be clean don away with speed by her Majestie and the parliament, meaneth to passe by us no more: but to suffer his whol displeasure to fall uppon us at his next comming. And in deed, as often as I consider our late defence from the Spanish invasion, together with our deserts, I am induced to think that the Lord then was affected towards us, as sometimes he was towards Israel his owne people, concerning whom he speaketh, Deut. 32. 26. I have said, I would scatter them abrod, I wold make their remembrance to cease from among men, save that I feared the fury of the enemie, lest their adversaries should wax proud, and lest they should say, our high hand and not the Lord hath done al this. Therefore let not our deliverance harden, you of the parliament, in the sinn of maintayning the breaches of the Lords house. The same Lord that wrought our deliverance, wil surely be the cause of our ruine, if his honor be so neglected by you as usually before time it hath ben. And we are to take heed, lest the Lord seeing our profane and vaine insulting of the victory, when we are not a whit bettered thereby, send some Jeremy among us which may cry, as he did unto the king and states of his time, in the like matter. Thus saith the Lord God of Israel, thus shal you say to the parliament of England. Behold, except at this your meeting, all the deformities that are tollerated in my service be at once done away, and except you grant free passage unto my gospel, the navy of the Spaniard which I discomfited before you, shal come againe, and fight against this land, and waste it with fire and sword. Therefore deceive not your selves, saying, the Spaniardes are so weakened by their last discomfiture, that they are not able to pursue their intended invasion, for it shal not be so. No, though you had smitten the whole hoste of the Spaniard that fought against you, and there remained but wounded men amonge them: yet should every man rise up in his tent, and overrun this land. And let us looke assuredly, whensoever the abject and contemtible enemy shall assaile us, abject and contemptible I say, in al respectes, in comparison of the value and strength of our men and munition (and the Lord increase them a thousand fold more) that this God, whose service is so litle estemed of us, wil send a terror into the hart of our valiantest and stoutest men, so that he, whose hart is as the hart of a lion, shalbe as weake as water: and on enemye shal chase a thousand of us, because the hand of the Lord wilbe against us for our sinns. It is not therefore the Spanish furniture and preparations: but the sins within the land, which we are most of all to feare. For although the army of the Spaniard were consumed with the arrowes of famine: although the contagious and devouring pestilence had eaten them up by thousands: although their totterting shipps were dispersed, and caried away with the whirlwinde and tempest, although madnesse and astonishment were amongst them, from him that sitteth in the throane, unto her that grindeth in the mill: although the Lords revenging sword, in the hand of our valiant captaines and souldiers, had so prevailed against them, as it had left none in that uncircumcised hoast but languishing and foyled men, notwithstanding a contemptible and wythered remnant of the plague and famine: a navie of winde and weather beaten ships, a refuse of feeble and discomfited men, shalbe sufficiently able to prevaile against this lande; unlesse another course be taken for Gods glory in Wales by your Hh. then hitherto hath bene. If I did speake unto infidels and ungodly atheists, I know I should not be so plaine, because unto such the trueth at sometimes is unseasonably spoken. But I speake unto those that have undertaken the profession of Christianitie, and therefore should at all times be fit to heare the trueth of God. And I know no temporising trueth, no temporizing judgements of God against sinne ; no trueth that is to be concealed unto christians, because their Hh. cannot brooke the same ; no trueth that is, eyther not at all, or minsingly to be uttered, because states love not to here thereof. So that I was in this matter, not to consider what your high places were content to here, but what was the dutie of your high places to heare. And therefore I should thinke it (I protest) an undutifull and flattering petition to entreat your Hh. not to be offended with mee for uttering the trueth. As though I supposed you would thinke it wonderful that a man should adventure to speake, even in the cause of his God, any farther then stood with your good liking.

The sum of all that the Lord requireth at your hands in the cause of his honour, is concluded in these 2. pointes. First, that you abrogate out of the Churche whatsoever you finde therein to be a breach of Gods ordinaunce. Secondly, that you countenance the preaching of the word, in such sort, as the course thereof be not stayed, for the pleasure or profit of any creature. These poyntes are so reasonable, that whosoever upon choise and deliberation denieth any of them (of inconsideracie and want of due examination of matters, I know many things may be done amisse) I cannot see what he differeth from a plaine atheist. And therefore againe I admonish you, in the name of God, to looke unto your selves, and thorowly to waigh what the Lorde by the mouth of Ezekiel threatneth against you, if you stil refuse his waies and mainteine these bypaths of mans inventions in his Church. You have feared the sworde, sayth the prophet, (Ezek. 11. 39 ; 10. 12) and I will bring a sworde upon you, sayth the Lord Jehovah, and I will bring you out of the middest of this land, and deliver you into the hands of strangers, and execute judgements among you. You shall fall by the sworde, and you shall know that I am the Lorde ; for you have not walked in my statutes, nor executed my judgementes, but have done after the manner of the heathen that are round about you.

The lawes, offices and officers of our church, for the most part, being not according to the statuts of the lord, but framed after the maner of the popish government, whereby the nations round about us are tiranized by the man of sin ; that is not a matter to be wondered at, that the alteration of our ecclesiastical state is desired. And, besides, our saviour Christ and his gospell came into the world, to alter yea and overthrow, states and governements, in al things wherin they should be contrary unto his wil, and I hope that you of this parliament will not deny him this prerogative. If I have sought the removing of anything, which the lord requireth not to be altered, I crave no pardon of mine oversight. What I have written in this whol treatise, I am ready by the grace of God, personally to make good (though it were uppon mine utmost peril) whensoever I shalbe thereunto called, by you of this honorable assembly, wherein there are many of good estimation and credit, who, upon the motion of mine appearance by this house, wil, I trust, undertake that I shall come to stand unto the premises by me set downe. So that I may obtain (which I most humbly crave of you, R.IIh. and worshipful) that upon mine appearance I be not by any court, or prerogative (only the H. court of parliament excepted, unto whom, as being the highest council in the land, in this cause I apeale) debarred of my liberty, before my cause according unto the word be overthrowne. The injury which I sustained the last parliament (being a suitor in this cause) enforceth me to crave this at your hands, which otherwise, I should have perswaded myselfe to be a needles suit. For whereas the auncient priveledges and liberties of this house, do give leave (during the parliament) unto any that are suitors thereunto, quietly to follow their suits without feare of any arrest, and being arrested, do presently deliver and set them free, I was not suffered to enjoy any the former liberties. But contrary unto all religion, law, equity, and conscience, to the great derogation of the liberties of this noble court, was committed close prisoner by some, who abused the high commission; their dealing might have appeared more tollerable, and lesse derogatorious unto your Hh. and worships, if they had shewed any cause of mine imprisonment (their abused authority only excepted) which unto this day is altogether unknowne unto me.

I know, that the infirmities and wants of men, who deale in good causes, are commonly beaten uppon the back of the cause they handle. Therefore the Lord knoweth how careful I have bin to keepe it unspotted, and myselfe out of all unnecessary danger. Setting downe nothing before I had considered what might insue, either in regard of the matter or manner of delivery. But why did I publish a matter of such waight, before I acquainted the parliament therewith? Whic it is published to the ende, that the parliament may bee acquainted with the suite, which could not be done by private writing. And it is but an ungodly shifte of those that would smother the trueth, to pretend it to be against the law, to move the parliament in any suit that is printed. As thogh the suits of men unto that high courte, were parliament statutes. Indeede, if the parliament had enacted the remooving out of Wales, all L.Bb., dumb ministers, etc., then were it an intollerable part for any to publish their actes, but by their appointment. Graunt you the petition, and the cavill of committing it to the presse will easily be answered. If you do not meane to yeeld unto the suite, neither woulde you have done it, being moved thereunto by private writing. The cause I make known, to the end it may be granted, and herein let not my life be precious unto me ; upon the necessitie of the publishing hereof I stand, because that the worlde may see when you redress these things, that you did nothing, that you durst leave undone, unless you would bring swift destruction upon yourselves and the whole lande. But what follie is it to thinke, that such great matters wilbe reformed in our dayes. Rather what injury doe they unto the whole state, who thinke that they wil any longer tollerate the breach of Gods law. And in this point, let the good opinion, that they who allege such pretences conceive, be wayed with my dutiful perswasions of this honorable assembly, and both causes judged accordingly. For mine owne part, I think the majestie of the cause to be such, as they who are the Lordes, dare not but entertaine it, and tremble to think, that all this while, it hath been so carelessly attended upon. And it is in the behalfe thereof, that I have presumed to deale with you, who otherwise durst nor have suffered my voyce to be heard, in the ears of the princes of my people. Let what I have written bee examined, yea, by mine adversaries themselves (if I have any) and it shal appeare that I have made a conscience, howe I have delt with my superiors, especially those concerning whom it is said, you are Gods, lest I should seem to leave behind me the least print of a minde in any sort tending to defame them or their governement. As I have bene carefull hereof, so let the Lorde, yea, and no otherwise (which I speak, as far as my corruptions will permit), grant this cause, and myselfe also, if it be his will, favour in your eyes. Indeed, in regarde of the cause, I come Mandatorie wise, unto this honorable assembly, but in regard of myselfe, I come in feare and trembling, as unto the Lords vicegerents, entreating most humbly, that the dignitie of so high a cause be thoght off, nothing the more dishonorably, because it is brought in my hands. And I protest, in respect of my sinnes, that the Lord may justly denie it the favour it deserveth in your eyes, because I am a dealer therein. But this should be no reason why the parliament should give it a repulse. For in the eyes and cares of al the world I make it knowne, that it is the cause of the living god wherin I deal, and that if it had been possible for me to have written more humblye and dutifully, I had done it. Or if I had seene anye waye that might have bene likelier to prevail with my superiors then this, I take the Lorde to witnesse unto my soule, that I would not have used this course. And I would to God I could tel how to make the cause plawsible. So farre I am, from setting downe anything that might carry with it any shewe of occasion to hinder and disgrace the same. Well, I have done my endeavour, the successe I expect at the

Lords hands, unto whome I commend the cause and the salvation of that poore people.

The sword of justice reached unto you by the Lorde himselfe, to take punishment onely of him that is an evil doer. I fear not, because I have not offended. If it should be drawne against me for this action, the president would be such, as they who meant hereafter to prophesie unto you, might be advisedly counseled not to prophesie, and the Lord, as a token of your just destruction to ensue, would say they shall not prophesie nor take shame. If I have spoken any untruth, beare witnes thereof; if a trueth, I dare stand to it by the Lords assistance, and demand what he is that will presume to object and throw himself unto the vengance of God, by punishing me an innocente; it is a common manner with some in these dayes, to threaten those who deale in this cause nowe in hand, but they are to know that it is not so easie a matter to spil their bloud, whose daies are numbered with the Lord. The Lord may (I may confesse with griefe) in regard of my other sinnes, bringe mine head to the grave with blood, but in this case what have I offended? And therefore undoubted woe wil betide him, that shall molest me for this worke. Howe sover it be, thus I have performed a duty towards the Lord, his church, my country, and you of this high court, which I wold doe if it were to be done againe, though I were assured to endanger my life thereby. And be it knowne, that in this case I am not afraid of earth. If I perish, I perish. My comforte is, that I knowe whither to go, and in that day wherein the secrets of all hearts shal be manifested, the sincerity also of my cause shal apeare. It is enough for me, howsoever I be miserable in regard of my sinnes, that yet unto Christ I both live and die, and purpose, by his grace, if my life should be prolonged, to live hereafter, not unto myself, but unto him and his church, otherwise than hitherto I have don. The Lord is able to raise up those that are of puerer hands and lipps then I am, to write and speak in the cause of his honor in Wales. And the Lord make them whosoever they shalbe never to be wanting unto so good a cause, the which, because it may be the Lords pleasure, that I shal leave them behind me in the world, I earnestly and vehemently commend unto them, as by this my last wil and testament. And have you, R. honorable and worshipful of this parliament, poore Wales in remembraunce, that the blessing of many a saved soul therein, may follow her Majestic, your Hh. and worships, overtake you, light uppon you, and stick unto you for ever. The eternal God give her Majestic and you the honor of building his church in Wales, multiply the daies of hir peace over us, bless her and you in this life, that in the life to come, the inheritance of the kingdome of heaven may be her and your portion. So be it, good Lord.

By him that hath bound himself continually,
to pray for your Hh. and worships.

JOHN PENRI.

www.ingramcontent.com/pod-product-compliance
Lightning Source LLC
Chambersburg PA
CBHW030907170426
43193CB00009BA/770